Disabled people and the Internet

Also available in the Digital Age series:

Wired for work? ICT and job seeking in rural areas
Ronald W. McQuaid, Colin Lindsay and Malcolm Greig

Internet use in sheltered housing: older people's access to new media and online service delivery
Maria Sourbati

Disabled people and the Internet

Experiences, barriers and opportunities

Doria Pilling, Paul Barrett and Mike Floyd

JR
JOSEPH
ROWNTREE
FOUNDATION
1904
2004

The **Joseph Rowntree Foundation** has supported this project as part of its programme of research and innovative development projects, which it hopes will be of value to policy makers, practitioners and service users. The facts presented and views expressed in this report are, however, those of the authors and not necessarily those of the Foundation.

Joseph Rowntree Foundation
The Homestead
40 Water End
York YO30 6WP
Website: www.jrf.org.uk

Rehabilitation Resource Centre

ISBN 1 85935 185 9   (paperback)
ISBN 1 85935 186 7   (pdf: available at www.jrf.org.uk)

A CIP catalogue record for this report is available from the British Library.

Cover design by Adkins Design

Prepared and printed by:
York Publishing Services Ltd
64 Hallfield Road
Layerthorpe
York YO31 7ZQ
Tel: 01904 430033; Fax: 01904 430868; Web: www.yps-publishing.co.uk

Further copies of this report, or any other JRF publication, can be obtained either from the JRF website (www.jrf.org.uk/bookshop/) or from our distributor, York Publishing Services Ltd, at the above address.

Contents

Acknowledgements

First we must thank the Joseph Rowntree Foundation whose concern for the exclusion of disadvantaged groups and whose grant made this research possible. We are very grateful to the Project Advisory Group, whose members were Tom Adams of the Office of the e-Envoy, Martyn Cooper of the Open University, Dianne Cockburn of AbilityNet, Mark Deal of Enham, Lizzie Eastwood of Arthritis Care, Guido Gybels of RNID, Mark Hinman of the Joseph Rowntree Foundation, Ruth Scott of SCOPE and Philippa Simkiss of RNIB, for their interest, advice and support. We are grateful to Mark Hinman for ably chairing the meetings, for liaising with the Foundation for us, for his general supportiveness and for inventing the original title of our project.

We are indebted to Guido Gybels of the RNID for his particularly detailed comments on our draft report. We must thank AbilityNet for allowing us to use telephone and email enquirers as the basis for our sample of disabled people, and Dianne Cockburn and Andrew Horrocks for facilitating the process for us. Without the help of many people the focus groups would not have been possible: we must thank Karen Garner of RNIB, Mark Deal of ENHAM, Alan Stacey of the 2000 Club and Ruth Scott of SCOPE for all their help in arranging these. Above all, of course, we must thank the people who completed questionnaires for us and those who participated in the focus groups.

1 Introduction

This project arose from a call by the Joseph Rowntree Foundation for proposals to explore how Internet provision of goods and services affects people's lives. While the Internet might have some intrinsic capability to provide goods, services and communication at a distance, improving access in doing so, some research findings in the early days of e-commerce suggested diminished access for some groups instead. The Foundation took the message from Jan Pahl's (1999) report *Invisible Money: Family Finances in the Electronic Economy*, that

> although e-commerce can bring advantages to people who are geographically isolated or excluded because of disability, people who do not have access to credit or information technology could become further disadvantaged as these forms of money grow, and as new electronic activities become the norm.

Subsequently, the Foundation commissioned a review of policy and research (Kingston, 2001) which indicated that the social implications of the Internet went beyond e-commerce and online shopping. This review paper also showed that there was much government initiative, particularly since Labour took power in 1997, to increase the variety of services and shopping available online. However, the paper suggested that there was insufficient attention to access issues, such as the obstructive cost of purchasing a computer and whether people could afford online connectivity.

The research presented here focuses on the impact of the Internet on people with disabilities. These are people who could potentially gain considerable benefit from using the Internet, but they are also likely to face difficulties in obtaining access to it for many reasons. These include the costs mentioned by Kingston, the nature of their impairments making computer use difficult – possibly requiring the use of special equipment or adaptations – and (for many) their general unfamiliarity with computers. There is also the possibility that provision of information and services through the Internet might actually narrow rather than widen choices, because it might lead to the phasing out of traditional ways of providing services preferred by some disabled people.

Methodology

The research methodology has three parts.

1 *The review*. A review of relevant research and other literature and information on the Internet including: the use of the Internet by disabled people and factors precluding its use; the extent to which UK and European policy initiatives on promoting use of the Internet take into account the needs of disabled people; a review of web accessibility initiatives; and the legal aspects of web accessibility. The review is to be found in Chapter 2.

2 *Questionnaire survey of views about the Internet of disabled Internet users and non-users*. This was carried out using a sample of disabled people who had made enquiries to AbilityNet's free telephone helpline or had emailed them for advice. AbilityNet is a UK charity that provides free information and advice on any aspect of computing to disabled people and a range of services for professionals and employers involved with disabled people. In 2001 there were over 23,000 telephone enquiries. Questionnaires were sent out for this research by AbilityNet to around 500 people who made enquiries on their own behalf, (AbilityNet preferring this method to preserve enquirers' confidentiality for their names and addresses).

It was decided to use AbilityNet as a base for the sample because it provided access to disabled Internet users over a wide geographical area. Our preliminary research review indicated that there had previously been very little research on the views and experiences of disabled people themselves in relation to the Internet. Most available evidence was anecdotal. The sample also provided access to non-users of the Internet, as not all computer users necessarily use the Internet, and AbilityNet's enquirers include people who do not have a computer but are seeking advice about getting one or seeking the funding to obtain one. It was recognised, of course, that this sample would by no means be representative of disabled people in general. Questionnaire findings are reported in Chapter 3.

3 *Focus groups*. To complement the questionnaire survey, and particularly because of the unrepresentative nature of the sample, it was also decided to hold focus group discussions. These focus groups were to have participants who were Internet users and non-users, to be people with a range of impairments, including economically inactive and older people, and to take place in different geographical locations. Eventually five focus group discussions were held. These are detailed in Chapter 4 of the report.

2 The review

Internet usage by disabled people

UK

Direct information concerning Internet usage by disabled people in the UK is scarce. Disabled people are not included as a separate group in the regular surveys on Internet usage that have been carried out by the Office of National Statistics (ONS). These surveys (e.g. ONS, 2002), as well as Oftel's (2002, 2003) nationally representative residential consumer surveys, show a very strong relationship between gross household income and home Internet access. Given the evidence for the lower income of households containing a disabled adult (Grundy *et al.*, 1999), it seems very likely from these figures that disabled people will have less Internet access than non-disabled people.

A few direct comparisons of Internet usage by disabled and non-disabled people do exist. In May 2000, when home access was much lower than it is currently, Oftel (2000) found that 17 per cent of disabled adults had home Internet access, compared with 25 per cent of non-disabled adults, but separate information for disabled people is not given in later surveys. A nationally representative survey in August 2000, commissioned by the then Department for Education and Employment (DfEE) (Research Surveys of Great Britain, 2001), found ownership of computers and the Internet considerably lower for disabled people compared with the total population. At that time, 32 per cent of disabled people were found to own a computer compared with 44 per cent of the total population, the figures for Internet access in the home being 19 per cent and 30 per cent respectively. Those with a disability specifically affecting computer use were also very much less likely to own a computer (23 per cent) than those with a disability affecting normal activities (35 per cent), the figures for Internet access in the home being 9 per cent and 18 per cent respectively. The survey also found that people with disabilities were less likely ever to have used a computer or the Internet than the total population. In a follow-up to this survey, commissioned by the Department for Education and Skills (DfES), carried out in November 2001 (Russell and Stafford, 2002), 36 per cent of respondents with a disability had ever used the Internet, compared with 55 per cent of the total population. However, the authors correctly suggest that the differences might be due to the older ages of those with a disability. There is an increase in the likelihood that someone will have a condition that constitutes a disability as they grow older, as the last national survey of disability in Great Britain in 1996/97 indicates (Grundy *et al.*, 1999): nearly half of the disabled population were aged 65 or older, compared with 21 per cent of the general population. Surveys of Internet use and home access have shown strong decreases with age. So the differences between the disabled and total population could possibly be due to the age difference.

USA

Data from the USA more definitively establish that disabled people are less likely to use the Internet than the non-disabled population. In 2002 the US Department of Commerce published a survey called *A Nation Online: How Americans are Expanding Their Use of the Internet*, which analysed September 2001 responses to the Current Population Survey – the first that included questions about specific types of disability in its set of computer and Internet use questions. The questions covered long-lasting severe vision, hearing, mobility and manual dexterity problems, as well as a question concerning any physical or mental condition that makes it difficult to leave the house.

To avoid the conflation of disability and age, the analysis was limited to three broad age groups: individuals under 25, 25 to 60 year olds, and those over 60.

Less than 2 per cent of the population between ages 3 and 24 reported having at least one of the disabilities specified.

- Between 8 and 17 per cent fewer of these disabled young people (according to disability type) had Internet access at home; up to 13 per cent fewer had Internet access at any location (probably school for most).

Among individuals between the ages of 25 and 60, the likelihood of having at least one of the five disabilities specified rose to 7.3 per cent.

- Between 7 and 19 per cent fewer of these disabled people used the Internet at home.

- Disabled people in the USA, as in Europe, have low rates of employment – but the survey also found that working disabled people who used computers in their jobs were up to 16.5 per cent less likely to use the Internet at work.

- People aged over 60 were less likely to be computer or Internet users; and those with disabilities were only half as likely to go online from home and a quarter as likely from some location other than home.

An earlier extensive survey by the US Department of Commerce (2000), *Falling Through the Net: Toward Digital Inclusion*, suggested that although the digital divide between rich and poor was narrowing, it persisted for disabled people. The information on disabled people came from the Census Bureau's *Survey of Income and Program Participation* (SIPP). The authors suggest that economic and demographic factors account for some but not all of the differences between disabled and non-disabled people.

Disabled people's attitudes to the Internet

Research evidence on disabled people's attitudes to using the Internet is scarce but what there is indicates positive attitudes. An evaluation of a Royal National Institute of the Blind (RNIB) project which devised a signposting system of educational and vocational guidance on the Internet found that visually impaired students stressed how hard it was for them to find information from a number of sources, and how much easier it would be if it were obtainable through the Internet (Pilling, 1997).

There are some individual accounts of the difference that access to the Internet has made in terms of choice and opportunities to be included in the social world (e.g. Porter, 1997; Farrow, 2003). Porter, who works at RNIB, points out that if newspapers are produced on Braille or tape for visually impaired people a lot of editing has already been done, but when they are available on the Internet the individual has the choice of what to read. Farrow, who used to be in the US Air Force before he was diagnosed with olivo ponto cerebellar degeneration and medically retired started selling lures for bass fishing online. He says that the Internet provides the opportunity to feel included and in touch with the world, and make an impact on the world.

These individual accounts are reinforced by findings of a survey of Internet use by disabled people carried out by Harris Interactive and commissioned by the US National Organization on Disability (NOD, 2001). Interviews were conducted online with 535 people who identified themselves as having disabilities and 614 who did not identify themselves as having disabilities. A notable finding from the survey concerned the Internet's perceived impact on quality of life for people with disabilities. Forty-eight per cent of the Americans with disabilities who connected to the Internet said that going online significantly increased their quality of life, compared with 27 per cent of the non-disabled people. Fifty-two per cent with less severe disabilities and 34 per cent with severe disabilities said that the Internet increased their ability to reach out to people who have similar interests and/or experiences, compared to 34 per cent of the non-disabled online Americans. Fifty-two per cent of the disabled interviewees said that the Internet helped them to be better informed about the world around them, compared to 39 per cent of the non-disabled interviewees.

A recent survey carried out by Leonard Cheshire (Knight *et al.*, 2002) found that 54 per cent of the disabled people in their sample considered Internet access essential, as opposed to only 6 per cent of the general population. Fifty-six per cent of the disabled population considered a home computer essential, compared with 11 per cent of the general population.

While the evidence available is broadly very positive on disabled people's attitude to the Internet, before the present study, research explicitly designed to determine the views and experiences of Internet users with a range of disabilities was very limited, particularly in the UK.

UK government online initiative

As indicated in the Introduction, one aspect of this review is to examine the extent to which UK and European Union (EU) policy initiatives in promoting the Internet take into account the needs of disabled people. The UK government is doing much work through the Office of the e-Envoy towards promoting the use of the Internet. According to the UK online Annual Report for 2002 (e-Envoy and e-Minister, 2002):

> The Government is committed to a radical reform of public services. The public sector has to rise to this challenge by providing flexible, responsive, high quality services. e-Government is a powerful catalyst to bringing about this transformation. Exploiting the opportunities new technology brings will allow Government to build services round customers' needs – and increase the efficiency of the end-to-end delivery process.

Central to this are two objectives:

- to make all government services available electronically by 2005, with key services achieving high levels of use

- to ensure that everyone who wants it has access to the Internet by 2005.

Getting government services online

At the time of the 2002 Annual Report 54 per cent of services were available online. As well as getting information, things that people could do online included:

- applying for Child and Working Tax credits

- submitting self-assessment tax forms

- booking and paying for a driving theory test

- getting health advice

- purchasing a TV licence

- finding out where roadworks are

- obtaining legal advice

- getting worldwide weather forecasts.

However, a 2002 international benchmarking study showed that while the UK has one of the most comprehensive e-government programmes and was one of only two countries to have an online target of 2005, the percentage using e-government services was low for individuals, though it was high for businesses.[1] This was despite the high level of connectedness among UK adults. Those countries with higher take-up had more user-centred services, or had prioritised services by their usefulness. To drive the programme forward, the government is now concentrating on key services, those where the potential for gaining significant benefits by 2005 – in terms of customer service and efficiency savings – is greatest. They are also striving to increase people's confidence in how personal data will be handled and in the security of the systems used, and to increase means of access, by, for example, extending the scope of services available via digital TV.

What is meant by efficiency savings?

The emphasis on efficiency savings through the provision of online government services raises the issue of whether the intention is eventually to end the provision of traditional services. If this were so, it could put disabled people, who appear very likely to have lower access to the Internet than the non-disabled population, at greater disadvantage than they are at present. This question is dealt with in the 2002 Annual Report, partially but perhaps not completely reassuringly. It notes that providing electronic alongside traditional services could potentially double the costs and goes on to say:

> although there may be short-term additional cost, we will realise the potential to make back-end processes more efficient, even if services are delivered through traditional channels. Additionally, as users switch to online access, departments may be able to make savings from the lower volume of transactions through conventional channels. In time it may be possible to switch some of these off provided that this does not disadvantage the service user.

Encouraging disadvantaged groups to take up online services

The 2002 Annual Report indicates that the government is well aware that there is a 'digital divide' in terms of lower Internet access among the most disadvantaged groups in society – those on low incomes, older people and disabled people. The report points out: 'These groups are traditionally heavy users of public services and potentially have most to gain from convenient, customer-focused channels of electronic delivery'. The government is taking a number of measures to increase usage, particularly among these disadvantaged groups.

Motivation

The report suggests that the greatest barrier to Internet usage is a lack of understanding of its benefits. This belief is derived from ONS findings that nearly half of the 43 per cent of adults who have never accessed the Internet gave a general lack of interest as their main or only reason for not having done so. Raising awareness of the benefits of online services and how to access them is regarded as one of the key means of overcoming the lower take-up of these groups. In November 2001 and January 2002 'Let's All Get On' adverts were run on (terrestrial) TV and on Sky Digital television to convey the message that the Internet is for everyone – regardless of age, ethnic group or background. In the monthly report for February 2002 from the e-Minister and e-Envoy (2002) to the Prime Minister, it was stated that a tracking exercise to the end of December 2001 showed this provided 'an encouraging start but there is still a lot to do'. While 'prompted awareness' had risen to 45 per cent of the population, 'spontaneous awareness' remained low, at around 3 per cent. A further major campaign took place in May–July 2003, dubbed 'Get Started' (originally the Online Nation campaign), which offered any individual a free Internet introductory session, and a variety of promotional initiatives were undertaken by partner companies and organisations, including the Royal National Institute for the Deaf (RNID). The 2002 Annual Report said that national advertising was to be 'at the heart' of the campaign, with TV advertising the best way to promote the message to socially excluded groups. In the event, however, there was no TV advertising. Instead, regional TV news and magazine programmes were encouraged to cover 'Get Started'; an online centre was also included in a *Coronation Street* storyline.

Access

In September 2000 the Prime Minister announced a target to set up 6,000 UK 'online centres' across England, to be based in community centres, public libraries and other convenient public locations. This target was reached by the end of 2002. Criteria to become an online centre include offering support to people with disabilities/learning difficulties. Centres must provide access 'where reasonable' for people with disabilities, and are asked on the application form how they are going to do this (DfES, n.d.).

A report is available on the early experiences of UK online centres situated in disadvantaged areas that receive funding from the Capital Modernisation Fund (CMF) (Hall Aitken Associates, 2002). Fifty-nine of the 580 centres opened in October and November 2001 were selected for the survey, and the report is mainly based on 1,360 questionnaires returned from users (24 per cent response rate). There were initial difficulties in the research because of delays in the opening of centres, and many of those included were not yet fully operational. It was found that 61 per cent of users were in the target disadvantaged groups,[2] including disabled people (8 per cent of respondents). However, 37 per cent of users said that they had home access to the Internet, which was very similar to the 38 per cent access in the ONS survey of July 2001. The authors concluded that the centres were not reaching the most socially excluded (poorest) groups, but that the information and communication technology (ICT) skill levels of users were low. Overall it is concluded that it was too early to assess the functioning of UK online centres, but a provisional recommendation was that managers needed more support in targeting and supporting more socially excluded potential users. There is no evidence on the availability of access for disabled people or special facilities for those who need assistive devices to use a computer or the Internet.

The 2002 Annual Report suggests that few people consider cost as a barrier to Internet usage. However, in the DfES study (Russell and Stafford, 2002), while half of Internet non-users said that nothing would encourage them to use it, the main incentives to use it were cost-related. Twenty-four per cent mentioned free/cheaper access and 13 per cent free/cheap lessons. Half did not have a computer and cheaper cost was again the main incentive to using one. In the Leonard Cheshire survey, 25 per cent of the disabled sample said that they could not afford a home computer. Cost is likely to be a greater disincentive for disabled than non-disabled people, as they generally have lower incomes, and may also have to purchase assistive devices as well as a computer.

The Annual Report does mention using the evaluation of the Wired Up Communities initiative (Devins *et al.*, 2003) to analyse the costs and benefits of offering home Internet access leasing schemes to the public. The most immediate aim of this project was to combat social exclusion by enabling most people in seven pilot disadvantaged communities to have access to ICT through a variety of technologies. Although complete 'wire-up' of the communities was not achieved, it seems to have been relatively successful in that just under three-quarters of those who received the technology used it to access the Internet and over 80 per cent continued to use it after the period of subsidy had ended. Non-use appeared to be related to the type of technology, such as the slow speed of set-top box technology or the unreliability of refurbished computers. Initial usage was lower in the area that did not provide free or subsidised initial access.

Access for disabled people

There are special measures for disabled people. Much effort has been put into developing the ukonline.gov.uk portal that gives access to all UK government information and services online using a single web address, and to making it easier to navigate and search. It is designed to provide access for those with visual impairments or low reading skills, and was awarded RNIB's 'See it Right' logo in February 2002. Guidelines have also been developed for government departments on how to make websites accessible for those with disabilities.

The 2002 Annual Report indicates that the DfES is developing a customised Internet search facility, provisionally called Cybrarian, due to be piloted in the autumn of 2003, which will facilitate access for those with physical, cognitive or sensory disabilities. Its aim is to provide access to a wide range of interesting content in a simple and accessible format, with easy navigation and step-by-step support. Determination of Cybrarian's usefulness must await the pilot's assessment.

Web accessibility

Accessibility has become a much greater issue for people with visual or motor impairments as computers are now able to handle intricate visual images – images which require subtle understanding by the computer user and fine movement controls such as with a mouse. This creates difficulties for people who are not easily able to see the graphics or associate them in the prescribed ways. Likewise, the fine movements needed on mouse or keyboard have created challenges for anybody with a motor or visual difficulty.

Having already become graphical rather than text-based, computers and the World Wide Web have rapidly become still more image-visual with Java applets (quickly downloadable small application programs in the purely object-oriented Java programming language). Unfortunately, many of the crucial images are not properly supported by descriptive text, limiting their effective use to (trained) people who can easily see, understand, point and click.

Assistive devices and software for computer operation have become available, but they have not benefited from the economies of scale (and competition) which have greatly lowered computer costs. An example of popular assistive technology is screen reader software, by which a synthesised voice articulates text displayed on a computer: when used for Internet access the screen reader depends on some knowledge of website layout and the availability of an accessible site. Even then, however, the best screen readers cannot 'read' images. The web designer must add text tag explanations for graphic images so that people using screen readers can move through the site.

A different problem exists for deaf and hard-of-hearing people when accessing audio and video content. While solutions to provide subtitling or textual equivalents (like SAMI[3] for instance) do exist, they are not being widely used and that means that an ever-increasing amount of content is not accessible for these users. Where screen readers can provide a (partial) solution for visually impaired people, current speech recognition technology is not capable of transforming free-spoken content into text. This means that providing such spoken content in an equivalent for deaf and hard-of-hearing people is required to make that content available to them.

Internet accessibility guidance – industry voices, W3C and the WAI

The World Wide Web Consortium (W3C), an international industry consortium founded in 1994 to develop common protocols and promote the web's evolution ensuring its interoperability (on different computing platforms), issues guidelines through the Web Accessibility Initiative (WAI, 2002) to promote accessibility for disabled people. It works in collaboration with disability organisations, research centres and governments and has identified the most common web design problems for people with particular disabilities. The *Web Content Accessibility Guidelines 1.0* (WCAG 1.0) has 14 points which summarise essential elements of accessible web design:

1   Provide equivalent alternatives to auditory and visual content

2   Don't rely on colour alone

3   Use markup and style sheets and do so properly

4   Clarify natural language usage

5   Create tables that transform gracefully

6   Ensure that pages featuring new technologies transform gracefully

7   Ensure user control of time-sensitive content changes

8   Ensure direct accessibility of embedded user interfaces

9   Design for device independence

10 Use interim solutions

11 Use W3C technologies and guidelines

12 Provide context and orientation information

13 Provide clear navigation mechanisms

14 Ensure that documents are clear and simple.

Attached to each guideline there are between one and ten checkpoints which interpret and specify the application of the guideline in website design.

The 65 checkpoints are graded between three priority levels giving an increasing standard of accessibility:

- Priority 1 is for checkpoints that 'a developer must satisfy otherwise some groups of people will be unable to access information on a site'.

- Priority 2 is for checkpoints that 'a developer should satisfy or else it will be very difficult to access information'.

- Priority 3 is for checkpoints that 'a developer may satisfy otherwise some people will find it difficult to access information'.

Adherence to the varying priority checkpoints defines three 'conformance levels':

- 'Single-A' includes Priority 1 checkpoints.

- 'Double-A' includes Priority levels 1 and 2.

- 'Triple-A' includes Priority levels 1, 2 and 3.

The WAI advocates that accessible web design benefits all users, non-disabled as well as disabled. For example, checkpoints that support web access for people with visual disabilities also help people accessing the web from mobile phones, hand-held devices, or car-based computers (when connection speed is too slow to support viewing images or video, or when a person's eyes are 'busy' with other tasks). Checkpoints such as captions support access for people with hearing impairments but also help people who are using the web in noisy environments.

The UK and web accessibility

As indicated previously, there are guidelines for UK government websites. They provide comprehensive information for building and managing usable and accessible websites. Requirements are for compliance with WAI level A and a number of additional guidelines (from Priority 2 and Priority 3) that have been judged best practice by the Office of the e-Envoy. It is stressed that design should be professional and attractive, that content should be plainly written, broken up into lists and easily scanned (e-Envoy, 2003a). There is also a consultation draft on guidelines for local government websites.

A number of projects aimed at exploring and developing new ways of implementing e-government were funded in the Local Government Online initiative (LGOL), which took place between June 2001 and June 2002. One of these, APLAWS (Accessible and Personalised Local Authority Websites) (2002), was a partnership between five London boroughs, private sector firms and voluntary organisations, including RNIB and Age Concern. It aimed to develop a standardised model for local authority websites to be accessible.

RNIB is a contributing member to WAI and is (with AbilityNet and the RNID) among 23 European organisations which launched a EuroAccessibility initiative in April 2003. RNIB and AbilityNet both provide information and consultancy in making websites accessible. In October and November 2003 RNIB held a series of web access seminars for web designers, working with AbilityNet in their delivery.

Despite the government commitment to accessibility, an internal report compiled by the Office of the e-Envoy found that nearly all of 65 central government websites were potentially excluding users (Cuddy, 2003). It is difficult to know how many non-government websites follow the WAI guidelines. The RNIB awards its 'See it Right' logo to websites it has audited and found reasonably accessible. Early in 2002 just four sites had been awarded the logo, but by October 2003 33 sites that had been audited in the past year had obtained it. However, there was a predominance of public sector and voluntary organisations. There should be better evidence available in January 2004 when the report of a 'Formal Investigation' of compliance with WAI accessibility standards by 1,000 public and private sector websites, commissioned by the Disability Rights Commission (DRC) and coordinated at the Centre for Human Computer Interaction Design at City University, London, is launched.

AbilityNet has started to review the top ten sites (by search engine ranking), in particular industry sectors quarterly, auditing them for accessibility and usability using the Bobby (v5) accessibility checking tool and a range of manual checks. In a first review of airline websites on a five-star rating from one star (very inaccessible) to five (very accessible), none reached the three-star basic level of accessibility, and only four attained two stars (AbilityNet, 2003a). Common problems were lack of labels for pictures and links, 'hard coding' of text size, so that it could not easily be made larger, and reliance on Javascript for booking a ticket, which many older browsers and some special browsers used by people with visual impairment do not support. Similarly in their second survey – of online newspaper sites – only three attained a two-star rating (AbilityNet, 2003b). It seems that disabled people are likely to be at a considerable disadvantage in accessing websites.

European Union policy for web accessibility

The European Union (EU) institutions promote inclusive accessibility for government websites throughout the EU, and maintain that most barriers could be overcome if web designers were to follow WAI rules.

At a symposium in April 2003, EU member states' ministers agreed that existing legislation should first be fully exploited but that new legislation should be considered to ensure inclusion and prevent discrimination for disabled people (European Union, 2003). They also called for the implementation of WAI guidelines in public websites.

A European Commission report (European Commission, 2002a) reviewed the status of EU public websites in following WAI guidelines and found that implementation had only just started in many member states. The Commission noted that it was powerless to demand change in commercial websites, but called on non-governmental organisations to lobby and monitor.

The Commission has also examined the application of legislation in member states to Internet accessibility and concluded that the current patchwork of member states' laws was weak (European Commission, 2002b). It recommended developing specific legislation at both European and national levels.

In June 2002 there was a resolution from the European Parliament calling for the implementation of WAI guidelines (Priority levels 1 and 2) on public websites (European Parliament, 2002).

There are several EU advisory groups working on this issue, including the High Level Group on the Employment and Social Dimension of the Information Society (ESDIS). This has contributed to a report (European Commission, 2002a) on the policies in programmes in different member states and has reviewed progress towards fulfilling the goal of inclusiveness.

Legal aspects of web accessibility

UK

Government guidelines, and those of other organisations, have drawn attention to the relevance of Part III of the Disability Discrimination Act (DDA) to website accessibility. The DRC revised Code of Practice (Access to Goods and Facilities and Premises) published in February 2002, and dealing with the duties placed by Part III of the Act, appears to strengthen its applicability, making explicit reference to provision of a website as a service which is subject to the Act, and also to an accessible website as a 'reasonable adjustment' that might be made (Adams, 2001; Mason and Casserley, 2001). However, the relevance of the Act to web accessibility has not yet been tested in a UK court case.

EU

The European Commission has examined the application of legislation in member states to Internet accessibility and concluded that the current patchwork of member states' laws was weak. It recommended developing specific legislation at both European and national levels.

USA

During the 1990s – particularly the latter half, while the Internet was growing exponentially – it was widely expected that it would only be a matter of time before websites would be legally challenged if they were not fully accessible to people with disabilities. Confidence that websites' designers would be compelled to improve accessibility was based on the

Americans with Disabilities Act (ADA) (US Congress, 1990) and also on the US Supreme Court's understanding that information access is an integral part of the First Amendment right to free speech in the US Constitution. However, a federal district court decided in October 2002 that a commercial website was not 'a place of public accommodation' and was therefore not covered by the ADA.

While commercial websites' obligatory accessibililty may now have to wait for more legislation through Congress, there is already legislation covering the public sector and all commercial suppliers to it. All government websites have to comply with the 1998 Section 508 amendment of the Rehabilitation Act 1973 (US Congress, 1998), which says that the federal government must make its information accessible to federal employees with disabilities and to the general public, unless this creates an unreasonable burden.

Conclusions

Findings from the USA suggest that disabled people as a group are less likely to use or have home access to the Internet than the general population and that this applies across the age range – to young people, 25 to 60 year olds and even the over-60s, who were less likely to use or have home access to the Internet than the other age groups. In the UK the only studies that give a comparison between disabled and non-disabled people are those on ICT use, commissioned by the DfES (and its predecessor the DfEE), and, as the authors themselves say, the different age distribution of the disabled population is not taken into account. So there is no evidence from the UK of the extent to which the disadvantage arises from age, or from being disabled, or whether all age groups of disabled people are equally disadvantaged.

Comparison between disabled and non-disabled people in terms of use of the Internet is actually more complicated than this. Access to the Internet, or even to services like the World Wide Web or email, by itself does not say anything about usefulness or usability. It might be that people with disabilities do manage to use the Internet, but that they are not getting an equivalent experience out of it and so are being disadvantaged. However, the little evidence there is indicates that disabled people who do use the Internet have positive attitudes towards it and this is supported by individual anecdotal accounts.

The government is undoubtedly very aware of the problem of social exclusion – including that of disabled people – but much of its strategy, on somewhat flimsy evidence, seems to be based on seeing motivation as the main factor deterring Internet use among disadvantaged groups. It seems that cost is dismissed as a reason for not having Internet access, but on the basis of their lower income alone, as well as the evidence from the DfES and Leonard Cheshire studies, it is likely that this might not be an inconsiderable factor for some disabled people.

There is undoubtedly considerable awareness by the government and local authorities in the UK of web accessibility issues, and a strong campaign led by RNIB and AbilityNet. How far this has penetrated private sector websites is difficult to say at present, though the AbilityNet surveys suggest it has not got too far. The large-scale study commissioned by the Disability Rights Commission to examine web accessibility is very much to be welcomed. While it seems that Part III of the Disability Discrimination Act is likely to cover website accessibility, this is yet to be tested in the courts. In the USA the ADA's applicability to commercial websites has been challenged, and there may be a need for specific legislation, as there was in the USA for government websites.

Before the present study, there appears to be no detailed UK research on disabled people's actual experiences of getting online, the problems encountered, the assistance required and received or not received, or of disabled people's views of the advantages and disadvantages of carrying out particular activities by this means. The present study goes some way to filling this gap. The questionnaire survey provides a considerable amount of information about use of the Internet by a particular group of disabled people (enquirers about computing problems to AbilityNet): their activities on the Internet, how they got it installed, how they learned to access it, assistive devices used, the assistance needed and obtained with these, and their views of its benefits and problems. It also specifically asks them about their knowledge of and opinions about the government initiative to put all services online by 2005. They are not a representative sample of disabled Internet users in the UK, but a group with mainly quite serious disabilities who want to use computers. Their views are supplemented by Internet users in four focus groups, with a range of disabilities, differing in computing experience, of varying age, employed and not employed, and coming from different locations in the UK. Not all the questionnaire respondents used the Internet, and four of the focus groups had non-users as well as Internet users, participants in a fifth focus group being all non-users of the Internet. The study thus also provides insight into the reasons deterring some disabled people from becoming Internet users.

Notes

1 Countries compared with were Canada, Sweden, the USA, Australia, Italy, Japan, Germany and France.

2 People who need help with basic skills; lone parents; people from ethnic minorities; unemployed people; disabled people; people over 60 not involved in learning activities.

3 SAMI stands for Synchronised Accessible Media Interchange, devised by Microsoft. It is a file format for accessible captioning and audio description for video material to be played on PCs in the Windows Media Player program.

3 The questionnaire survey

Sample

The findings presented in this chapter are drawn from questionnaire responses of a sample of enquirers to AbilityNet over a six-month period. AbilityNet is a UK charity which gives free advice and information about any aspect of computing to disabled people. Enquirers can call a free telephone line or email. The sample was limited to individual enquirers only.

It is important to emphasise that the sample is not representative of disabled Internet or computer users. AbilityNet enquirers were a 'convenience sample', being a readily available source of disabled people with experience of using computers and the Internet, or seeking to do so. As remarked in the review section, there is almost no previous published research asking British disabled people about their experiences with the Internet. AbilityNet enquirers cannot be generalised to all disabled Internet users but the views of these respondents can give a valuable insight into how disabled people use the Internet, and how they see its advantages and disadvantages, opportunities and challenges.

Selection of sample

AbilityNet posted 508 questionnaires in mid-July 2002, with reminders being sent to those who had not completed the questionnaires in mid-September. One hundred and ninety-six completed questionnaires were eventually received (three respondents were excluded for not being disabled people; 13 people explained why they could not complete questionnaires). The valid response rate was 39 per cent.

For recruitment, AbilityNet was asked to take a random sample of 35 per cent within each functional disability category of individuals who had made telephone or email enquiries to AbilityNet over the previous six months. However, some categories were oversampled where these groups had made relatively few enquiries to AbilityNet – oversampled groups were those with hearing, speech and mobility problems, and people with learning difficulties or dyslexia. In setting the disability categories, those with upper limb disorders were combined with those reporting problems in operating the keyboard/mouse group as being likely to have similar difficulties. There was a similar rate of response from people in the various categories with perhaps some slight under-representation of those with learning difficulty or dyslexia.

Characteristics of sample

It was not possible to obtain the functional disability categorisation given to the 193 individual respondents by AbilityNet because of the need to preserve personal confidentiality. However, the questionnaire asked 'How would you describe your disability?' and 'How does your disability affect your use of computers?'

Table 1 has been constructed from answers to the questions on disability. This indicates that hand/arm problems were the predominant functional disability (5 per cent were repetitive strain injury – RSI), with visual impairment as the next most common. Those categorised in Table 1 as 'Problem not defined' indicated that their disability did affect their use of computers, but did not relate how it did so. Others described their disability, but did not answer the question on how it affected their use of computers, and they were categorised as 'No problem indicated'. Some respondents specifically stated that their disability did not affect their use of computers, and they are categorised as such in the table. These included people with a variety of disabilities, including mobility problems, myalgic encephalomyelitis (ME), multiple sclerosis (MS), mental health problems and a speech problem.

Mobility is only included in Table 1 if it was said to give rise to a problem with computers, and a much higher proportion, almost a quarter of respondents (43), had a mobility problem. The numbers mentioning sight problems (44) or hand/arm problems (92) are also higher than Table 1 indicates.

In the last survey of disability in Great Britain (Grundy *et al.*, 1999), disabilities of locomotion were the most common, affecting 72 per cent of the sample, while just over a third had disabilities of dexterity (35 per cent). Dexterity problems were unusual among those with mild levels of disability but very prevalent among more seriously disabled people. While this suggests an under-representation of people with mobility problems in the present study sample, and that the sample is inclined to the more seriously disabled, differences in questions asked about

Table 1 Main functional disability affecting computer use

	No.	%
Hand/arm problem (including repetitive strain injury – RSI)	78	42
Registered blind/severe visual impairment + other disability	22	12
Other visual impairment	14	8
Dyslexia/dyspraxia	10	5
Learning disability	3	2
Aphasia/dysphasia	3	2
Aspergers	3	2
Concentration, memory problems	3	2
Mental health problems	3	2
Difficulty sitting	7	4
Mobility problems	3	2
Pain/fatigue problems	9	5
Problems with monitor	4	2
Multiple	1	0.5
Problem not defined	8	4
No problem indicated	5	3
Computer use not affected by disability	10	5
Total	**186**	**100**

disability and in age structure mean precise comparisons cannot be made. RSI is also probably more common in this sample than among the disabled population as a whole.

The 65+ group (16 per cent) is small in the present sample, compared with 48 per cent in the last survey of disability in Great Britain (Grundy *et al.*, 1999). There were also low numbers of respondents between 16 and 24, probably reflecting the low disability rate in this age group and also the fact that they may have gained familiarity with computers at school. Almost half the respondents (48 per cent) were aged between 45 and 64.

The respondents were almost equally divided into males and females. In the disability survey in Great Britain there was a slightly higher proportion of women (54 per cent) in the adult (16+) population.

The long-term nature of the disability of the respondents in the present study is notable, almost three-quarters (73 per cent) having been disabled for more than five years and 53 per cent for more than ten years.

Respondents were also asked about their employment status. The very high number of respondents who were not working because of illness or disability, 78 (42 per cent), is striking. Another 53 (28 per cent) said that they had retired, ten of these in the 35 to 54 age category, explicitly saying that they had retired owing to ill health. Only 22 (12 per cent) respondents were in paid employment, nine of these being in part-time employment. Fourteen (8 per cent) were at school and three at college.

Use of the Internet

As would be expected of enquirers to AbilityNet, the majority of respondents, 136 (71 per cent), had used the Internet, but there was a sizeable proportion who had not gained access. Proportions using the Internet were very similar for males and females. Internet usage was lower for the 65+ group (55 per cent) than for the other age groups (73 per cent).

However, the Internet usage pattern was very different from that in the general population. The Office of National Statistics Omnibus surveys (e.g. ONS, 2002) show a steady decline with age. In October 2002 the rates were: 94 per cent for the 16–24 age group; 79 per cent for the 25–44 age group; 68 per cent for the 45–54 age group; 47 per cent for the 55–64 age group and just 17 per cent for the 65 and over group.

Internet activities

Respondents were asked which activities they used the Internet for, and when they had first and most recently used the Internet for these activities.

Taking last use as the most accurate account of whether respondents had used the Internet for particular activities, over 90 per cent used email and almost as many (85 per cent) the World Wide Web. Chatrooms, Instant Messaging and newsgroups were used far less often, each by fewer than a fifth of the respondents.

Three-quarters of those who used email had done so in the last seven days, the figure being only slightly lower for World Wide Web users. Around a third of those who used email or the World Wide Web had been using the Internet for these activities for one to three years. However, substantial numbers (42–45 per cent) had been using it for these activities for less than a year, and a good proportion of these had started use only in the last month. It is, of course, at the start of use that problems are most likely to arise and this may be why AbilityNet was contacted (although enquiries were not necessarily related to Internet usage).

Nearly all Internet users had used it for their private or personal use (96 per cent). Just under half of those personal Internet users used it for this purpose only. About a quarter (33 users) had used it at some time for work, a quarter (32) for a college or university course, and under a fifth (23) for another educational or training course, while 19 had used it at school.

Aids, equipment and adaptations

Around two-thirds (89) of the respondents who used the Internet said that they needed special aids, equipment or adaptations to use it (also referred to as assistive devices in this report).

Almost half (45 per cent) of the Internet users who needed assistive devices specified that they needed voice recognition to use a computer or the Internet. Over a quarter said that they needed keyboard adaptations (28 per cent) and just under a quarter (24 per cent) mouse adaptations. Around a fifth needed speech output systems, mainly screen readers, but two people used text readers because of reading difficulty. Other adaptations needed were magnification or special colours, with a few other items of equipment or adaptations being mentioned such as a special chair, armrests or software for dyslexia.

Respondents were also asked about the availability of assistive devices, if needed, and support for using them. While the majority (70 users, 78 per cent) of respondents who considered that they needed assistive devices did have aids, equipment or adaptations available, almost half (30 users, 43 per cent) of these had problems with them. Another ten did not have available what they thought that they needed, and four were awaiting an assessment or looking round for what they needed.

Availability of assistive devices

Those respondents who already had the assistive devices that they needed usually had these devices in their own homes. However, four respondents said that the assistive devices were only available for them in other locations (work, school, a community organisation, a nursing home).

Several of those with home-based assistive devices were people who worked at home. One said that he depended on voice recognition for his business. One or two had obtained the equipment through Access to Work. One self-employed person said that she needed:

> Ergonomic mouse+keyboard. Voice activated programme etc. Extra large monitor.

And that she had obtained

> Brilliant support from Access to Work. Best I've had from my (multiple) uses of various services.

However, another respondent, who had also received various aids and equipment at home, including a voice recognition system, through Access to Work, was critical of the service, because it had not also provided the training that she needed.

Respondents who said that they needed assistive devices were asked if they had experienced a lack of availability of these or of support in a variety of locations other than their homes.

One respondent, with spinal problems, commented about the public library:

> Plastic chair only, on which I cannot sit. I cannot stand to access. Only short pre-booked slots available. No voice activation, therefore need to type.

Another, who used voice recognition, said that she had been interested in an adult education course, but was told that a suitable computer was not available for the course as it was part-time.

Disabled people and the Internet

A partially sighted respondent who used magnification software said:

> I would love to use an Internet café as my own computer often breaks down. I cannot access Internet café's computers.

Problems experienced with assistive devices

Voice recognition systems (VRS)

Considerable problems were experienced with voice recognition systems. One respondent set out the problems:

- the time that has to be taken sitting reading from a set text

- having to correct in a special window

- the microphone having to be at exactly the same angle each time

- problems if voice tone not the same each time

- instructions being in the machine and not on paper.

She had found it all so difficult that she had virtually given up.

There were numerous references to the problems of using voice recognition systems with the Internet:

> Speech input doesn't work properly with all Internet sites.

> Find the voice activated very tiring to use re www. Dragon Dictate not always recognising words – irritating and wearying.

> I suppose my voice is not consistent enough for it.

Even a respondent who taught ICT had problems:

> I use IBM ViaVoice Millennium Professional Edition at home for word processing long documents. Although on the whole it's a good package it can really bug me when it can't recognise words and can

be a bit awkward. Although it can be used for Internet surfing the amount of effort required is counterproductive so I just use a laptop with a touchpad which gets me away from the mouse.

Screen readers

There were also considerable problems with screen readers.

One respondent said:

I've recently bought a screen reader – but I keep getting error messages. It doesn't read emails or the Internet. When I receive emails I save them and enlarge.

Another said:

I've now got version 5 Hal but it doesn't read everything.

And another:

JAWS does not cover all of problems experienced in using web. So I have to use other people to help me as well.

Keyboard and mouse

Few respondents who needed a special keyboard or mouse mentioned problems, but one respondent with rheumatoid arthritis said:

Yes I need to use an on-screen keyboard and an easier-to-use mouse but have not been able to get one and so use computer very rarely.

and in answer to the question on problems experienced:

I have extremely weak arms and hands and find the mouse difficult and I have tried a few at AbilityNet but few helped. The ones I bought prove difficult after a short period of use and returning them can be difficult and it's too expensive to keep buying new and to try. Somewhere that lent them in one's own home to try would help.

Another solved their problems after a visit to AbilityNet (see below).

Magnification

One respondent who used large magnification could only see four words at a time, and found this very awkward. Another said:

> My son is 10 years old and newly registered blind and has only used the Internet a few times. He has Supernova as an aid but I feel it is not good enough for continuous Internet use. Supernova does not seem to give a clear picture or point on the Internet – it looks a bit fuzzy when it's blown up.

A respondent using Lunar said that he could not access websites.

Help with adaptations

Many respondents expressed the need for good advice but only a few had experienced its effectiveness. One respondent, who had severe arthritis, would have liked to use the Internet more, but said:

> Have tried various sources for support and advice to make computer easier and less stressful for joints which are painful.

A respondent who said that she was partially sighted had had no problems with the adaptations needed because she had had sufficient help:

> Computer has been programmed to display large text (yellow) and symbols on black background, also a Reader. I was assessed at AbilityNet who provided me with details they recommended – this was given to supplier who programmed my computer accordingly.

Another respondent solved their problems after a visit to AbilityNet:

> Joystick had never been really suitable and only after a visit to AbilityNet was advised of alternative use of mouse.

Another hoped that their problems were solved:

Postural difficulties prevented my full use of my computer. The extremely adjustable screen on the new Mac and a new chair with adjustable back will I hope lead to more comprehensive use of my computer. It was difficult to find out what improvements I could make … the interview with AbilityNet was helpful in finally deciding to make the purchase of the new computer and chair.

Another respondent had JAWS at home, but was experiencing difficulty in using it at the time of completing the questionnaire:

Without the software there is no access for blind people. JAWS is a specialised software which needs a knowledgeable person to provide support.

However, when telephoned to clarify a point on the questionnaire, this respondent said that she had managed to find a charity which sent someone to help at home, and had become much more comfortable with it.

One respondent had received social services training on screen reader software but the centre did not have Internet access and did not solve her home problems.

Another respondent needed Zoomtext at the time of completing the questionnaire. She had subsequently obtained funding from social services, but now needed help to use it.

Cost of assistive devices

One respondent who had had a spinal injury said that a computer he could use would make a tremendous difference to his life. He would need:

Voice-activated dictation, and also a head mouse and, as I'm confined to bed a lot, a laptop.

He said that he had tried to get the adaptations he needed about three years ago, but the problems were financial. Someone from AbilityNet came down. 'They can tell what is available, but you still have to get.'

Another respondent with a severe spinal condition, a wheelchair user, responded that:

> Special aids would be a tremendous help to me. Such as an adjustable height desk, roller mouse, ergonomic keyboard.

and then

> The aids I mention above would need to be purchased by myself. I am unable to work and can't afford them.

Cost forced compromises on the adaptations respondents needed. A visually impaired respondent with a very small amount of vision used a special colour scheme, large mouse and XP Narrator (talk-back software for long text). He said:

> XP Narrator is half-way stage. It's better than nothing. But it leaves a lot to be desired on the Internet. If I had the money, I would have JAWS.

Another respondent said in relation to aids/equipment or adaptations needed:

> VRS helps but I have the most basic system. If this cost could be reduced, a more elaborate and sophisticated package could be purchased. Need a good VRS system, but unless you are employed it's difficult to obtain. I am trying to use the computer to obtain professional employment.

Some did manage to find funding. A respondent with musculo-skeletal problems having a voice recognition system said:

> Funding would have been a problem but for generous charitable assistance.

Views of websites

Websites and use of assistive devices and disability

There was a strong relationship between the need to use assistive devices and website accessibility: only 38 per cent of those needing these devices found most or many sites easy to use and navigate, compared to 69 per cent who said that they did not need them. The difference between the groups is probably sharper than indicated in Figure 1 – 15 Internet users did not reply to this question about websites, some specifying that their experience was too limited to do so, and ten of the 15 needed assistive devices.

Respondents with sight problems had significantly greater problems in finding accessible websites.

Views of how to improve websites

Respondents were asked to suggest ways in which websites could be better designed for easier use. Around 40 per cent of Internet users did so, with varied suggestions, having several recurrent themes.

Figure 1   **Opinions about websites' accessibility for Internet users who need and do not need assistive devices**

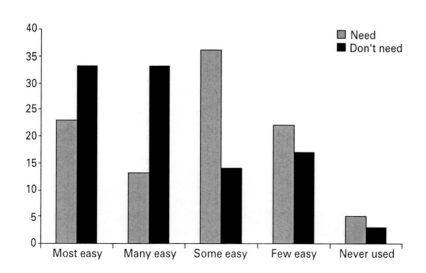

Disabled people and the Internet

The most common themes were for sites to have guides on the home page as to what is on them, for pages to be less cluttered, for fewer graphics and advertising, for links to be clearer and fewer, for print size and colours to be easily changeable to suit the user, for greater standardisation, for search to be more clearly marked and more precise, and for better accessibility for voice recognition system users.

Guides to sites

Respondents wanted home page information with a summary or index listing contents and clear navigational instructions, without too many links:

Summary of information on the site.

Clear index with no page more than 3 clicks (links) away.

Website tuition as you log onto the sites, showing you around …

Better layout and highlighted … guide you step by step.

More guidance on basic navigation needed.

Clear signposting.

Less cluttered pages

For example:

Simplicity is the key.

More succinct.

Less crowded visually.

Less waffle.

Fewer graphics and advertising

For example:

Less global advertising e.g. you log onto a site but before you can see their home page some 'special offers' blurb pops up.

Less pictures.

Too many flashy graphics obscure the text.

The adverts are highly annoying.

One respondent suggested that if there had to be graphics they should be on one side, text on the other. The screen reader would not read them if they were intermixed and she gets lost.

Graphics are also seen as annoying as they make for slower downloading.

Clearer and fewer links

For example:

Get lost in maze of links – only Dolphin, Guide Dogs and dedicated sites are good.

Clearer links down one side to get to different sections would improve some sites.

Colour and print size

Several respondents asked for larger print size, and colour that allowed background to be distinguished better from text, or to suit their needs, such as:

Clear and large – no yellow or red.

Standardisation

Respondents wanted standardisation both within and between sites on such matters as headings and the input of personal information:

I often miss items placed in non-standard (unexpected) areas, such as LOGOFF etc.

It would be even better if an agreed format could be used across organisations, e.g. BBC, government and commercial.

Search

Respondents wanted search facilities to be easier to find; they wanted to be guided about what search terms to use and they wanted search results to be precisely relevant. A typical response:

Make clear where on the screen the thing searched for is to be entered (typed). Make clear what to do to launch the search.

Problems with voice recognition

Have found this difficult with voice-activated and hence not used Internet much. Mostly email.

More voice friendly. Some don't let you scroll up and down with voice.

Links that can be activated by VR.

Other suggestions

Three respondents, two with reading difficulties and the other who was blind and had a physical disability, would like sites to read out their content:

Put voices on them – make them speak.

Other things that respondents would like sites to do:

Indicate clearly when one should wait.

[be written in] more plain English.

Provide information about products without starting the shopping process.

Use with keyboard shortcuts.

How people learned to use the Internet

Almost half of the Internet-using respondents were at least partly self-taught; a quarter were entirely self-taught. The high proportion (44 per cent) who had received help in learning from a friend or relative is notable, suggesting that those who do not know someone else who uses the Internet are less likely to start using it. There was a tendency for Internet users aged 55 and over (54 per cent) to be more likely to be taught by friends than younger users (39 per cent). Just under a quarter of respondents (33 users) had taken a training course. A few others had had some training with equipment, such as a voice recognition system, but said this was not a 'course'. Almost all (88 per cent) of those who had taken a course had done so on their own initiative, rather than from work.

Searching the Word Wide Web and emailing were the most common activities for training (received by almost four-fifths of those who went on training courses). Almost 40 per cent had had training in the use of special aids, equipment or adaptations. Training received was rated quite highly (three-quarters rating training as useful or very useful), though its scope was often quite limited. Training for special aids/equipment or adaptations was particularly appreciated but several respondents commented on problems because adaptations were not available on equipment at their training venues.

Over 40 per cent of Internet users had not taken, but would have liked, a training course. They were asked what had prevented them. One-third had difficulty in finding a course locally. One-third had difficulty in finding facilities for people with sensory impairment in local courses. Respondents found courses advertised for free but which lacked any suitable facilities for their needs, or suitable specialist software but nobody to train them with it. About a quarter of users said disabled persons' physical access was a problem and almost a quarter mentioned cost. Another problem mentioned by several respondents was the difficulty in getting to a course, either because of their mobility problems and/or the difficulty of travelling to it.

This respondent's comments illustrate these difficulties:

> I'm housebound without help to attend courses. They don't have adapted computers in this area on courses I did check on. I could possibly have got my husband to take me to an evening class but not over a long time as he has enough to do with work and looking after me.

Several people said that they needed a flexible course, as their health problems might mean that they could not attend regularly. Two parents (replying on behalf of children) had looked in vain for a children's course in their area.

One respondent commented on their difficulties in finding a course like this:

> I would like to use Apple equipment, but all courses seem to use Microsoft.

> Many courses are first floor – difficulty with lift arrangements or no lift at all.

> Cost can be rather high.

> Course specifies beginners but most of the class definitely not in this category.

Making more use of the Internet

Internet users were asked whether they would like to make more use of the Internet. Two-thirds (87 users) replied that they would like to do so.

By far the most common reason given, from almost half of those who would like to make greater use of the Internet (47 per cent), was the fear of high online call costs:

> I am with NTL on 1p a minute – so this restricts my usage. It is only £10 per month but my wife would worry about bills – we are pensioners.

The problems of the cost of assistive devices have been seen earlier in the report, and were the reason given for not using the Internet more by over a quarter (28 per cent) of respondents. Around a quarter (24 per cent) gave the cost of buying their own computer as a reason for not using the Internet more.

One respondent who was saving to buy a computer said:

> It is so important and useful to disabled people in helping them to communicate, access information, services and goods and retrain for employment that there must be more direct financial assistance.

Around a fifth gave the difficulty in finding advice on assistive devices as the reason for not using the Internet more. About one in eight said that their disability prevented them from making more use of the Internet. Frustrations in use, lack of time, and 'lethargy' were also given as reasons by several respondents.

Personal use of the Internet

Where respondents used the Internet

As might be expected, the 130 people who accessed the Internet for their personal use mainly did so at home (84 per cent). However, substantial minorities used it in other places: at another person's house (18 per cent), an educational institution or school (17 per cent), a library (14 per cent) or a community or voluntary organisation (7 per cent). Only 9 per cent went online at work.

Two-thirds accessed the Internet at one location only, but around a fifth accessed it at two locations, and more than one in ten at three or more. Nevertheless, this study's respondents were generally less likely to go online at places other than home than the general population. Figures from the ONS Omnibus survey for July 2001 (ONS, 2001a) indicate that 33 per cent accessed it from another person's home, 36 per cent from the respondent's workplace, 24 per cent from school or another educational institution, and 8 per cent from a public library. The particularly marked difference in workplace access is due to the high rate of economic inactivity among disabled respondents in the present study.

Disabled people and the Internet

The higher use of the public library among respondents to the present study is interesting.

Respondents were asked which location they used most and over 80 per cent said this was at home. Around 40 per cent said it was convenience, but about 20 per cent said that they were housebound or had mobility or other disabilities which made getting out difficult. Almost a quarter said it was because this was where their assistive devices were and they were not available elsewhere. The two respondents who used their workplace most said that this was because there was better access there, including voice recognition in one case and broadband in the other. Four used the library most, saying this was because it was free and in one case because support was available.

How often respondents used the Internet

Respondents who used the Internet for their personal use were asked how often they accessed it.

Internet-using respondents were online more than the general population. Seventy-six per cent of men and 62 per cent of women used it more than once a week, compared with 58 per cent of men and 48 per cent of women in October 2001 (ONS, 2001b). More of the respondents than the general population were also online daily (men 43 per cent and 26 per cent daily respectively; and women 25 per cent and 18 per cent respectively).

What respondents used the Internet for

Respondents were given a list of possible Internet activities, and asked to indicate for which of these they had accessed the Internet. Replies are given in Table 2, as are comparisons with the ONS Omnibus survey for the dates nearest to those when this survey's questionnaires were completed (ONS, 2003).

Comparison with the ONS survey for these dates indicates that the particular disabled population in the present study is not too different from the general population in the purposes for which they use the Internet except that respondents seem to be greater users of government and official websites.

Table 2   Internet activities of respondents, compared with those in ONS surveys

	Respondents %*	ONS survey 7/02 %*	ONS survey 10/02 %*
Using email	86	78	76
Finding information on goods and services	71	79	71
Buying or ordering tickets/goods/services	40	46	44
Personal banking, financial and investment activities	29	30	28
Looking for jobs or work	11	22	23
Downloading software including games	31	**	**
Playing or downloading music	12	19	23
Finding information related to schoolwork or an educational course	40	31	36
Using or accessing government official services	36	16	16
General browsing or surfing	62	57	54
Other things	21	4	4
Total no. respondents	**130**		

*   Percentages do not add up to 100 as more than one activity could be carried out.
**   Question was asked differently in ONS surveys at these dates.

'Other things' covered a considerable variety, mostly being information-finding.

Respondents were asked which activities they carried out most often. Emailing was overwhelmingly dominant, well over half giving this as one of their main activities.

Respondents were also asked open-ended questions on what they found were the main advantages of using the Internet, from which a consensus emerged. Speed was the advantage first mentioned by over a quarter of the respondents, with convenience of carrying out activities from home and ease of communication and the wide range of information each being mentioned by about one-fifth of the respondents:

Email is instant and easy to use. The use of the Internet for other activities gives access to a huge amount of information.

Convenient. Large library of resources at my fingertips.

The ability to carry out these activities in my own home and instant efficient access to information and entertainment.

Other themes were the benefits for people who were housebound, or had disabilities which made writing or reading ordinary print difficult or impossible, or the sheer difficulty in finding some kinds of information in other ways:

Quick and saves letter writing as writing is not easy for me as my hand function is not good.

More information easily available ... email quick and easy for writing to people – I can read text on my PC (right colours) but am unable to read paper format.

... saves me writing (I have problems with this), also easier than verbal communication (problems here also).

... because of disability – computer enables access to vast quantities of information.

Not being able to use a phone verbally this is the best way to communicate. People on the other end do not know I'm disabled.

How activities were carried out before having Internet access

Before gaining Internet access, around 60 per cent of users said that they used conventional methods, phone and letters for keeping in touch with people or to find out information, and a range of other sources, including TV, radio, magazines and books, for further information. About a quarter also visited other information sources, mainly the library:

Library, literature sent off for, and letters which took ages to wait for.

With physical difficulty and worry! The effort prevented me from doing other things.

A blind respondent said:

I used Braille a lot, and listening to tapes. The Internet is much better, it gives independence – don't have to ask.

More than one in ten relied entirely or mainly on others, usually relatives or friends. A respondent with a visual impairment said:

> It was very difficult. I don't know how I managed before – I had to ask other people and get them to read. It's nice to do for yourself.

However, another respondent pointed out that the Internet may not overcome problems entirely:

> I had to rely on friends/family – I still do as Internet has limitations.

A quarter, like this blind respondent who said she was dependent on JAWS, replied to this question on how they had carried out these activities before with 'I didn't', or that they had done so only to a limited extent.

Why the Internet was not used for some activities

Those who did not buy goods or services online were asked the reason for this in an open-ended question. By far the most common reason, given by around 40 per cent of respondents to this question (59 users), was security. The next most common reason, given by almost one-fifth, was that they preferred other methods – they liked to be able to see what they were buying. About one in ten said that they lacked the skills or knowledge of how to do this or were still learning. Other replies were each given by a few respondents – that they did not have a credit card, that they had problems with their computer or did not have easy access to one, that the process was too complicated, that they had problems reading the sites with assistive devices, that the delivery process was unreliable or took too long, or that they were on too tight a budget to buy online.

Asked why they did not carry out other activities online, by far the most common answer, given by over 40 per cent (65 respondents), was that they had no need to or were not interested.

Overall advantages and disadvantages of using the Internet

Respondents were also asked about the main advantages and disadvantages in using the Internet in two open-ended questions. Advantages focused around a few recurring themes, as indicated above.

Responses about disadvantages were much more diverse, though about a quarter can be categorised around the theme of the Internet being slow, cumbersome, difficult or time-consuming to use. Expense was seen as an important disadvantage, mentioned by about one in six. Having to sift through irrelevant information was an annoyance to about one in ten. Physical strain, which is likely to be a more prominent feature for disabled than non-disabled Internet users, was also quite often mentioned.

This respondent sums up a number of problems:

> Time-consuming. Potentially expensive. Difficult to find one's way around … Physically painful and tiring to use keyboard, joystick mouse, etc. I could go on.

Other disadvantages, each mentioned by several respondents, were security issues, web accessibility problems, junk mail and viruses, and isolation.

Almost one in ten said that there were no disadvantages.

Accessing the Internet from home

Most (85 per cent) of those who used the Internet for their personal use were or had been previously able to access the Internet from home. Of these the vast majority (92 per cent) had their own computer and generally used this. Two usually accessed the Internet via digital TV. Two usually used someone else's computer.

Assistance in installing Internet access

Friends and relatives were overwhelmingly the main source of help with installing access to the Internet at home (for 48 per cent of respondents). Other sources of help were AbilityNet or the supplier/installer of the computer (each for about one in ten respondents), with smaller numbers obtaining help from a course, magazine, charity, manual or Internet Service Provider (ISP).

Respondents were asked whether the help they received was adequate. Almost two-thirds said that it was, and another fifth that it was partly so. Nevertheless nearly two-thirds said that they would have liked some additional help. Not everyone was specific about the kind of additional help that they needed, but the most common demand (by around one-sixth) was for continuing assistance, with a clear and simple manual, and a telephone line with expert help, either free or at local cost (around a tenth of respondents), coming next. This respondent said about the help initially received (from installer and his wife):

> Sufficient to get started, but as time goes on need ongoing help to overcome difficulties/problems which continually arise … e.g. how to change third colour on sites so I can read them.

Another wanted

> a simple idiot-proof guide on how to do anything on the Net. I've just got an *Idiot's Guide* and it's difficult to read and written in jargon.

Around a tenth also wanted specialist help with using assistive devices (voice recognition, screen reader, keyboard rather than mouse) for access:

> Help from a knowledgeable person who knew how to use JAWS.

> To understand access without a mouse – there's not enough information on this.

Respondents were also asked whether they had had problems when they initially tried to access the Internet from home. Just under a half (48 per cent) said that they had had problems. Most of these problems were those that anyone has when they first connect (not being sure what to do, 'teething problems', 'learning', difficulties in getting a connection, becoming disconnected, not knowing how to use a search engine), but a sizeable minority were related to disability or the use of assistive devices. One respondent, for example, had problems when his ISP upgraded Netscape, which was not usable with keyboard access. He had to change to Internet Explorer.

Respondents were asked whether they still had problems in accessing the Internet, and 44 per cent said that they did. Again, many of these problems are quite general (problems in connecting or staying online being the most common, with web searching also still being a problem). However, over a quarter of the still-existing problems appear to be connected with disability. A respondent who had both dyslexia and dyspraxia said:

> Can't find my way round, become confused, require hard printouts to follow sites, and that is yet far too difficult.

The Internet non-users

The 56 Internet non-users were asked why they did not use the Internet.

By far the most common reason was cost (40 per cent), in most cases this being given as a general answer, but the cost of buying a computer, the cost of online access and the cost of adaptations or equipment needed were also specifically mentioned.

A respondent who lived in a nursing home following a stroke said that they had two state-of-the-art computers but not the adapted keyboard and mouse that he needed, and that he had been trying to raise funds from charities for these without success. Another said he had been trying to obtain grants for JAWS and training to use this for six months, and although he'd obtained some it was not sufficient, and that the grants run out if not claimed.

Need for training and for the right adaptations, or for the adaptations they had to work properly, were important reasons for not having Internet access:

> I have impaired vision, and despite my attempts to receive tuition I have never succeeded in receiving any. Thus, I am reluctant to purchase a computer, unless I am certain that I shall be able to use it.

Only a relatively small proportion (15 per cent) said that they were not interested in using the Internet, or had no need of it.

Internet non-users were also asked if there was anything that would make them more likely to use the Internet in the future. In line with the above, by far the most common answer, by over a third of those answering this question, was more cash, or funding to buy a computer, or the aids and adaptations needed. Nearly a third gave obtaining suitable adaptations. Training was the next most frequent response. Only six respondents said that nothing would make their use of the Internet more likely.

Just under half of these respondents did have a computer, though a few said it was too old or not suitable. Again Internet non-users in this study are not representative of disabled people who do not have Internet access, because they had approached AbilityNet, sometimes about how to obtain funding for a computer. But the responses do indicate that this is far from being the only problem.

Views of the government's UK online campaign

Overall, just over a third of respondents had heard about the government's UK online campaign. As Figure 2 indicates, there was little difference in the proportion knowing about this between Internet users and non-users.

Figure 2   **Proportion of Internet users and non-users who knew about the government's UK online campaign**

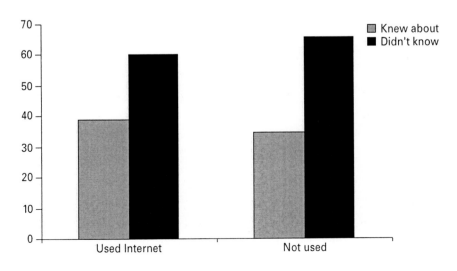

Few, only around one in ten, knew where their local UK online centre was, the proportion being slightly higher for Internet users (11 per cent) than non-users (7 per cent).

Respondents were also asked whether they thought it a good idea for the government to make all its services available online. A vast majority, over 85 per cent of those who replied to this question, answered positively. Respondents were asked to comment on this question and quite a number did so. A few comments were unequivocally favourable:

It is good because it will give each person independent access to the service that they want to find out about.

However, a number who replied affirmatively also had reservations, mainly that alternative communication methods would be phased out and those who did not have access to a computer would be excluded:

But not <u>exclusively</u> online.

With the proviso that it does not make others without it second-class citizens.

Yes, but should still provide alternatives for people who haven't got/ can't use Internet, i.e. phone/text phone, written format, audios etc.

One or two suggested that the government should provide computers for everyone:

Everyone should have the facilities to be online. Otherwise you don't feel part of the community.

One or two who were not in favour of all government services being online had similar views:

Not a good idea. It would increase the gap between those who have against those who are in the bottom league.

If all services [are] made available online this would inevitably become government's preferred means of communication. Therefore traditional means would become more difficult and resources reduced.

Another fear was about the potential loss of personal contact:

> If all you are looking for is info then 'yes'. Experience tells me that services are only ever dealt with satisfactorily on a personal level.

Security and privacy were also concerns:

> Providing they don't make contacting a human being more difficult, or ask personal questions in such an open medium.

Discussion and conclusions

The questionnaire received a 39 per cent response rate which is above the average rate of around a third for a postal questionnaire. The sample is reasonably representative of enquirers to AbilityNet although, as we deliberately oversampled some groups, it slightly under-represents those in the largest functional disability group, categorised by AbilityNet as having keyboard/mouse problems. It is not, as has been stressed, representative of the disabled population. It is likely to be biased towards the more seriously disabled.

It is not surprising that, given the nature of computing, hand/arm problems predominated among enquirers to AbilityNet. The high proportion who said that they needed (though they did not necessarily have) voice recognition is more surprising. Again, given the sample base, it is not surprising that almost two-thirds of the sample who used the Internet said that they needed assistive devices to do so. The clear association between the need for assistive devices and ease of understanding and getting round websites is a major finding of the study.

Lack of needed assistive devices impeded some respondents' Internet use away from their own homes. Several respondents used library and community facilities and more wanted to use community-based locations if suitable facilities and support were available at them.

Problems with assistive devices were a recurrent theme, particularly with voice recognition systems. Several respondents had found them so frustrating that they had given up using them. Among the common problems, voice consistency proved over-challenging.

Disabled people and the Internet

Screen readers appeared less frustrating, but imposed initial operating problems, and again when software updating was necessary. Magnification systems were sometimes problematic but keyboard and mouse adaptations aroused fewer complaints.

Respondents who used the Internet were asked to comment on how websites could be better designed for easier use. While most of the suggestions would not be new to those familiar with the W3C WAI guidelines, they certainly reinforce the need for their implementation.

Training was an important issue for these respondents. Forty per cent would have liked a training course, but could not find a suitable course locally, or there were no special facilities for people needing assistive devices, or they could not afford the cost, or were prevented by disabled access difficulties. Some people could not get out to a course, and a need for more home training to be available is indicated. There was also much need for continuing guidance when problems arose, and while telephone help (provided it was not too expensive) was adequate for some, it was not for everyone. Friends and relatives played a significant role in helping respondents both to install Internet access and to learn how to use it. Disabled people inexperienced with computers, and without computer-experienced friends or relatives, appear unlikely to start themselves.

Internet-using respondents appeared to be online more often than the general population, a finding in line with that of the US NOD/Harris study (NOD, 2001). Speed, the convenience of carrying out activities from home, ease of communication and the wide range of available information were the main Internet benefits mentioned. The Internet enabled social contacts and information-finding for some who had been previously prevented by their disabilities, or who had to rely previously on friends and relatives.

Costs were a significant issue to Internet-using respondents. Two-thirds would have liked more Internet use but felt that costs of online access were the main reason preventing this. Costs of buying their own computer and costs of buying assistive devices were reasons given by almost a quarter. Cost was the most common reason given for not using the Internet by non-users, including the cost of buying a computer, of online access and of assistive devices.

The vast majority of respondents were in favour of the government making all its services available online. However, there were strong reservations, mainly related to alternative traditional services being phased out and those without access becoming second-class citizens.

While the survey's respondents cannot be accepted as typical of the disabled population in general they do indicate an eagerness to use the Internet by many people who have considerable difficulties in accessing it. The survey also identifies certain help needed to prevent disabled people becoming more socially excluded in the 'Internet age'.

4 The focus groups

Composition of groups

Five focus group discussions were held, all groups except group 4 consisting of both Internet users and non-users:

1   older people with visual impairments living in Nottingham who had taken part in RNIB's project 'Campaigning for the Future'

2   mid-life working-age men with mild physical disability on vocational training course at ENHAM, Hampshire, an organisation providing employment-related programmes for people with disabilities

3   mixed group of younger and mid-life people with learning and physical disabilities, some of whom were wheelchair users, on development programmes at ENHAM

4   mixed group of mid-life and older people with diverse moderate disabilities from a west London sports and social club, some living in sheltered housing

5   mixed-age group of fairly experienced Internet users, mainly recruited through the newsletter of Scope, the national charity.

As with the sample of questionnaire respondents, the focus groups affirmed that disabled people are a heterogeneous group – Internet access presents numerous difficulties for some and few for others.

Internet interest

Whereas the questionnaire respondents were all enquirers to AbilityNet, and therefore people who had made enquiries about computing, the focus group participants were not necessarily people who had any experience of computing. It is notable, therefore, that nearly all these people were interested in using the Internet.

- The vast majority, whether already experienced with the Internet or not, ranged from being fairly to very interested in the Internet, believing it to hold benefits for communication, information or entertainment.

Typical areas of interest were in websites for general information-finding, for home shopping and websites tied to TV programmes. While specific interests varied individually, focus group participants who were Internet non-users or low users identified the main attraction in accessing the Internet as the huge and varied information available on the World Wide Web.

While Internet non-users and low users recognised the attraction of email, focus group participants with more Internet experience were enthusiastic about email, which is consistent with the questionnaire findings and the ONS Omnibus survey (Chapter 3, 'What respondents used the Internet for').

Opinions about the safety and convenience or attractiveness of e-shopping or e-banking were mixed. Participants generally maintained that disabled people are more anxious than the general majority about online fraud, danger and privacy issues. With respect to shopping online, this also mirrors the comparative findings of the questionnaire and ONS Omnibus survey.

Access to computers

Many participants expressed the wish for more or easier availability of computers and Internet connectivity. One focus group developed a strong consensus that people with acquired disabilities fare much better with computer use if they happened to have learnt computing before the onset of their disability.

People who had not got computers, and who were not Internet users, usually did not know the costs of computers.

- All agreed that perceived computer cost was an important factor in influencing them whether or not to have their own computers, but all heavily overestimated the cost of computers, although the real current cost of computers would still probably have been severely challenging for most participants.

- All those who did not possess their own computers knew (and evidently envied) other people who had their own PCs.

These findings corroborate those of the questionnaire (Chapter 3, 'The Internet non-users') with respect to the importance of perceived computer cost. Like questionnaire respondents also, very few focus group participants knew of computer availability at libraries or UK online centres. All those who did know had encountered severe difficulties in physical access to the location and/or other difficulties, such as with the unavailability of suitable assistive devices. No single focus group participant had succeeded in gaining satisfactory regular access to a publicly available computer for Internet access.

Of those who had ever accessed the Internet, all were certain that they would use a computer often if they could get access to a machine easily and without cost.

Access to the Internet

In spite of the challenges of computer access, nearly all focus group participants still wanted Internet connectivity, or wanted more Internet access if they were able to be online (with their own PCs, for example).

- Focus group participants who were Internet users believed that they would be online much more than they were currently if they did not have to pay telephone time charges, or if unmetered access were cheaper.

- Most Internet non-users wished that they had an Internet-connected computer available within easy access for trial and use.

Access to training – both for computer use and for Internet access

Reflecting the high interest of most focus group participants in the Internet, people who were non-users to date were highly motivated to find Internet training and to be online, even if they had previously had bad experiences in finding general computer training.

- All focus group participants believed that training was essential to get proper use of the Internet.

- Nearly all agreed that they would like occasional, cheaply available or free, unpressured training and guidance with computers, from which to explore the benefits of the Internet or to use it better.

Computer novices needed encouragement as well as training, it was widely believed. Computers and the Internet were associated with jargon and/or incomprehensibility by which it was easy or inevitable to be confused. Manuals should be written in simple English without jargon.

- There was very little knowledge about the training provided by UK online centres or through other organisations. Training outreach of government centres, local libraries and voluntary organisations was poor.

- All agreed (both current Internet users and non-users) that training had to be appropriate to individual needs, rather than 'generalised' or targeted to seemingly irrelevant outcomes: training for the Internet should therefore be individualised and specific, relevant and responsive to a particular learner's wishes, needs and methods.

The 'success rate' of computer or Internet training could not be measured in the focus groups, whereas three-quarters of the questionnaire respondents who had managed to receive Internet training did rate it quite highly (Chapter 3, 'How people learned to use the Internet'). However, the sentiments expressed in the focus groups strongly suggested that good training could only extremely rarely be found, reinforcing the findings of the questionnaire survey, where 40 per cent of Internet users would have liked but did not manage to find suitable training. Overall findings suggest that disabled people might have difficulty or meet obstacles in identifying and securing competent computer and Internet training, but, if appropriate training could be found, they prove to be successful and fairly satisfied pupils.

Assistive devices

Focus group participants who had any experience of assistive devices were unanimous about having difficulties identifying what to use, in affording it (if for personal use rather than use at work) and in getting guidance or training with the equipment. This is consistent with the survey's findings (Chapter 3) from respondents who were generally more computer-experienced than the focus group members, suggesting that there are substantial difficulties confronting disabled people at all levels of computer expertise.

One focus group (of mixed Internet users and non-users) concluded that assistive technology aids were generally so extremely expensive that they were nearly always too costly for individuals unless they were employed and paid for by Access to Work.

The focus group with the greatest proportion of experienced computer and Internet users wanted to recommend that keyboard shortcuts (usable for either operating systems or for particular programs) should be more publicised and better taught. They also believed that:

- More assistive features should be available within operating systems, instead of as special extra software and hardware devices. They should be standard features on all computers, providing useful facilities for all users, rather than created for users deemed to have special needs.

- Windows operating systems' accessibility options were not fully known or understood by many disabled people. Many simple additional helpful changes to computer operation are available by awkward or obscure manoeuvres through inconspicuous menus – and are therefore unknown to many disabled people. Good guides to the full range of 'accessibilising' possibilities would be invaluable.

Further focus group findings

Two further striking findings arose from the focus groups, unconnected with the specifics of access, affordability and training or communication, information and entertainment – one negative, one positive:

- While Internet-based information becomes ever more widely available, these focus group participants were extremely anxious that information might also become secluded and exclusive by being only available to people with easy access to the Internet, unimpeded by reliance on any special adaptations or devices.

- Computer operation for Internet access evidently gave the diversity of disabled people in the focus groups – people from diverse backgrounds, ages and situations – a strong, enduring and satisfying sense of achievement with some feeling of independence, no matter what their prevailing circumstances.

5 Conclusions and recommendations

The main purpose of this study is to determine whether the Internet will provide opportunities for many disabled people to carry out activities which they were previously unable to do – or could only do with difficulty – or whether it will lead to greater social exclusion.

Undoubtedly the questionnaire survey has confirmed that the Internet opens up many possibilities. This comment, added at the end of a respondent's questionnaire, is a graphic illustration:

> Internet is the *only* method for a tetraplegic for private communication … Internet is the *only* way for a tetraplegic to shop.

Despite many difficulties in finding the advice and assistance that they need, many of the respondents to the questionnaire make good use of the Internet. Others would like to make more use than they do, but are hampered by problems with assistive devices – finding the most suitable, the cost of buying the most effective, learning to use them. Many would make more use of the Internet except for other cost worries about getting and being online.

Disabled people may have stronger needs for or benefits from the Internet than the general population, but they have a lower usage rate (although definitive data are needed to verify this indisputably). Disabled people's needs will become more urgent as the government approaches its target of putting all its information and transactions online. Questionnaire respondents generally welcome this, but are fearful of lack of alternatives – for situations where personal communication is needed – and particularly for others who cannot afford to get online, or have other difficulties in getting online. While the government proclaims that alternative 'traditional' services will be retained as long as necessary, it is hoped that lower demand for these will allow savings, which could make traditional services more difficult to obtain.

Recommendations to government
- Commission nationally representative survey of computing experiences and requirements of disabled people.
- Ensure that traditional ways of providing information and services are and remain available for those who need or want them.

The government is certainly very aware that there are groups – including disabled people – who may become socially excluded if they do not have Internet access. It is also aware of the web accessibility needs of some disabled people. However, the government overemphasises motivational factors as inhibiting access while largely ignoring practical factors. The main exercise to narrow the 'digital divide' in 2003, the 'Get Started' campaign (originally the 'Online Nation' campaign), offered a free introductory Internet session for anyone who wanted it. The message of the campaign was carried by 17 'partner' organisations – some of whom were more aware of the real issues. Gordon Lishman, Director General of Age Concern, said in the press release (e-Envoy, 2003b) for the campaign:

> While older people stand to benefit most from the IT revolution, they are less likely than younger groups to get online. The reasons are not straightforward and may include insufficient income, difficulties with vision and hand movements, or a perception, if they did not use IT at work or school, that IT is not relevant to them.

Despite the government's original emphasis on motivational factors in planning 'Get Started', matched by its declaration that it would promote Internet access through TV advertising, the actual campaign appears to have been fairly low key and diffuse, with some off-peak TV editorial coverage (in regional news and magazine programmes) and one peak-time reference to an online centre in a *Coronation Street* storyline. The summary evaluation of the campaign (e-Envoy, 2003c) found that 16 per cent of those calling the helpline for more information were disabled, which is below the proportion of disabled people – one-fifth – in the adult population in the latest study of disability in Great Britain (Grundy *et al.*, 1999).

Apart from web accessibility, the main measure targeted at groups specifically including disabled people appears to be the 'Cybrarian' concept, due to be piloted at the end of 2003, an easy-to-use and potentially exciting Internet search facility. While this might increase the motivation of those who are able to try it out, it is not going to solve more fundamental problems of obtaining long-term Internet access for those who do not have, do not know where to obtain advice about and cannot afford assistive devices, or those who need training to use a computer, cannot afford a computer, or are worried about or cannot afford online costs. Nor will it help those who do not have friends and relatives to help them set up Internet access. It is these practical problems that need to be solved.

Awareness of the existence of local UK online centres among disabled people was low before 'Get Started'. Only 10 per cent of questionnaire respondents, and even fewer of the focus group participants, knew the location of their nearest centre. Moreover, some questionnaire respondents pointed out the difficulty of finding UK online or other training centres where assistive devices, and a staff member trained or experienced in teaching people how to use them, were available. It is possible to find out the location of centres by entering a postcode on the UK online website, and there is also a phone number for locating centres. Information about locations and about the phone line are less easily available to people who cannot yet connect to the Internet and see the UK online website. All such information needs much more prominent publicity through other media. The questionnaire survey findings suggest that disabled people are disadvantaged by the difficulty of obtaining information about special facilities as well as the apparent scarcity of those facilities.

Recommendation to government
- Create effective publicity for a central telephone resource that can provide information on the location of UK online centres, details of travel to location, access to buildings, facilities available at them and expertise of staff.

The early UK online centre evaluation suggested that centre managers themselves needed more support in both attracting and supporting people in the disadvantaged target groups. This certainly seems likely to apply to disabled people, who have very varied needs and often need individualised training. From April 2003 the University for Industry (UfI), the organisation behind learndirect, has been asked to support and develop UK online centres. They are aiming to extend resources developed in relation to disability for learndirect to the UK online centres. UfI has also obtained European Social Fund (ESF) funding to enable AbilityNet to provide support to learndirect and UK online centres in disability access audits, equipment demonstrations and assessments with individual learners, and to help promote the centres to disabled people. There is also a helpline available to centres taking queries about disabled access. It is essential that the reach and effectiveness of these services should be evaluated. Consideration should also be given to developing training certification for UK online trainers.

Recommendations to government
- Evaluate UK online centres' operations for availability of access and assistive devices for disabled people, for staff qualified to teach people to use them, and for effectiveness of support offered in relation to disability and disability access.
- Develop a training certificate for trainers at UK online centres and elsewhere.

The questionnaire survey indicates that, for some disabled people, home is the only place where it is feasible to obtain training. In London there is an organisation, U Can Do It, that offers training at extremely reasonable prices. While there are some other charities that provide training in the home they are not widely known – they also tend to be overstretched, even without wider publicity. Commercial home training is very expensive.

Recommendation to government
- Give funding and other support to voluntary organisations which provide home computer/Internet training for disabled people.

Recommendation to charitable trusts
- Help to fund organisations which work to improve disabled people's access to the Internet.

There is also need for greater promotion and resourcing of organisations that can give information and advice on assistive devices. Questionnaire responses and the focus groups both showed that disabled people have difficulties in identifying sources of information, guidance and training in relation to assistive devices. AbilityNet recommends training from the supplier for anyone who buys a voice recognition (VR) system, but many questionnaire respondents evidently lacked sufficient training, and/or may have bought systems without understanding enough about their suitability or usability.

Recommendations to government
- Give funding support to organisations which provide information to disabled people on assistive devices.
- Give cash grants for at least part of the cost of assistive devices to disabled people on benefits or low incomes.

Recommendation to web designers
- Build greater understanding of the needs of those using assistive devices.

Recommendation to manufacturers of assistive devices
- Consult more closely with disabled people concerning practical operational problems.

Voice recognition is still a far from perfect technology. In general, as yet, VR systems can work well within very strict constraints: quality of the audio input, the user's accent, the small size of the applicable grammar (lexicon), etc.

Screen reader users also had initial difficulties and needed continuing support as the systems updated. Like other assistive technology, screen readers can be very expensive and there are examples among the questionnaire respondents of people who both managed and did not manage to obtain funding from charities. Some made compromises and did not obtain what they really needed because of cost.

While the government clearly acknowledges web accessibility issues, these appear less often heeded by most commercial organisations with websites. Questionnaire respondents indicated many ways in which websites could be improved, including summary of contents on the home page, clear navigation guides, simplicity, less advertising and graphics, clearer and fewer links, more instructions on how to search – all reinforcing the need for wider implementation of the W3C WAI guidelines. These in themselves do not guarantee usability (particularly at the WAI A level), and user testing is also necessary. Commercial organisations need to become aware of the implications of the DDA for web accessibility. The DRC's large-scale study of web accessibility is very much to be welcomed: both the DRC and the government should lobby commercial organisations on this issue. Findings are due early in 2004, and a website usability competition would be timely (like one launched in 2000 by the National Autistic Society and City University, but with greater publicity).

More and better dissemination of information should be available about accessibility options and adjustments available for computers, operating systems and programs. Questionnaire findings suggest that some respondents were unaware of these. Even participants in our last focus group, who were experienced Internet users, were not aware of much that is possible. There is a need for plainly written manuals containing such information, as well as a guide to initial Internet access. Age Concern has a good beginners' guide, but its title of *How to be a Silver Surfer* might be off-putting for some. Downloading information from the Internet is obviously inadequate for people who are having difficulty accessing it.

Recommendations to voluntary organisations
- Produce an easy-to-understand introductory guide to the Internet, suitable for users of all ages.
- Produce an easy-to-understand manual about all the accessibility adjustments that can be made on a computer.

Although computers have decreased in price, cost was still a major problem for some of the questionnaire respondents, and an important reason for limited or no use of the Internet. Knowledge of organisations that provide recycled computers, and greater encouragement of this, might help to mitigate the problem, although the experience of unreliability from the 'Wired Up Communities' project suggests that this is only a limited solution. Cost of online access was a significant problem for many questionnaire respondents, and one raised in the focus groups. The importance of cost factors to disabled people is consistent with other studies (Knight *et al.*, 2002; Russell and Stafford, 2002). Subsidised costs, for those on benefits and low incomes, could be an important way of encouraging greater Internet usage. Cost of assistive devices can be greater than the cost of computers, and a government subsidy for those on benefits or low incomes should be considered here too.

Recommendations to government
- Introduce and promote a scheme for providing free or subsidised computers and online access in a larger variety of locations, including sheltered housing, where they may be easily accessed by disabled people.
- Subsidise online subscription costs for disabled people on benefits or low incomes.
- Devise and promote incentives for organisations to recycle computers (provided that they conform to acceptable working standards).

Disabled people and the Internet

The enthusiasm of people to join this research study's focus groups supports our view that disabled people are generally not lacking motivation to get online. Rather, encouragement, ease of access and easily available individualised training appear to be strongly needed.

The UK online 2002 Annual Report gives much space to a discussion of Internet access through a variety of channels, and perhaps there is an underlying idea that existing problems may be solved when everyone has a digital television. As an RNIB report (2002) points out, a screen reader has not been developed for digital television and at the moment people with visual impairments cannot use it to access the Internet. People with other disabilities may well have problems in manipulating digital television. There is also still the problem of the cost of subscription packages. The RNIB report says:

> While developments such as digital television bring huge potential for deepening and extending the social, economic and cultural inclusion of disabled people there is also a danger that in reality many will be excluded from benefits altogether. (RNIB, 2002, p. 13)

This is true generally about Internet access – but it would not take too much practical help from the government for the outcome to be one of greater inclusion.

Recommendation to government
- Address problems of accessing the Internet via digital television for visually impaired and other disabled people.

We also urge the government to
- Extend the 'Access to Work' scheme to disabled people not in work, so that they can acquire computer and Internet expertise for prospective employability.

... and urge the Disability Rights Commission to
- Lobby commercial organisations on web accessibility and usability issues.
- As part of its campaigning, to launch a promotional competition for the most accessible and usable website.

References

AbilityNet (2003a) *State of the eNation Report, July 2003 – UK Airlines.* Available online (accessed 10 December 2003) at: http://www.abilitynet. org.uk/content/oneoffs/Airlines%20eNation%20report.pdf

AbilityNet (2003b) *State of the eNation Report, November 2003 – UK On-line Newspapers.* Available online (accessed 10 December 2003) at: http://www.abilitynet.org.uk/content/oneoffs/Newspaper%20eNation%20 report.pdf

Adams, T. (2001) *Website Accessibility and Usability: A Summary.* London: Office of the e-Envoy, Cabinet Office

APLAWS (Accessible and Personalised Local Authority Websites) (2002) *Pathfinder Final Report.* Available online (accessed 10 December 2003) at: http://www.aplaws.org.uk

Cuddy, I. (2003) 'Disability laws force redesign of almost 800 government websites', *eGov monitor Weekly.* Available online (accessed 10 December 2003) at: http://www.egovmonitor.com/newsletter/w73/ ln01.html

Department of Commerce (2000) *Falling Through the Net: Toward Digital Inclusion.* Washington, DC: US Department of Commerce. Available online (accessed 10 December 2003) at: http://search.ntia.doc. gov/pdf/fttn00.pdf

Department of Commerce (2002) *A Nation Online: How Americans are Expanding Their Use of the Internet.* Washington, DC: US Department of Commerce. Available online (accessed 10 December 2003) at: http:// www.ntia.doc.gov/ntiahome/dn/

Devins, D., Darlow, A., Petrie, A. and Burden, T. (2003) *Connecting Communities to the Internet: Evaluation of the Wired Up Communities Programme*, Research Report No. 389. London: DfES. Available online (accessed 10 December 2003) at: http://www.dfes.gov.uk/research/data/ uploadfiles/RR389.doc

DfES (Department for Education and Skills) (n.d.) UK online centre criteria, Information sheet B. London: DfES. Available online (accessed 10 December 2003) at: http://www.dfes.gov.uk/ukonlinecentres/ downloads/2364_Information_ sheet_B.pdf

Disability Rights Commission (2002) *Disability Discrimination Act 1995 Code of Practice (revised). Rights of Access: Goods, Facilities, Services and Premises.* Available online (accessed 10 December 2003) at: http:// www.drc-gb.org/uploaded_files/documents/2008_223_drc%20cop%20 rights%20of% 20Access.doc

e-Envoy (2003a) *Illustrated Handbook for Web Management Teams,* Section 2.4. Available online (accessed 10 December 2003) at: http:// www.e-envoy.gov.uk/Resources/WebHandbookIndex1Article/fs/ en?CONTENT_ID=4000092&chk=XHiT3L

e-Envoy (2003b) 'Drive to encourage new Internet users unveiled'. Available online (accessed 10 December 2003) at: http://www.e-envoy.gov.uk/MediaCentre/CurrentPressReleaseArticle/fs/ en?CONTENT_ID=4000122&chk=QZI%2BZP

e-Envoy (2003c) *Summary Evaluation of 'Get Started'.* Available online (accessed 10 December 2003) at: http://www.helpisathand.gov.uk/news/ 2003/get-started-evaluation

e-Envoy and e-Minister (2002) *UK online Annual Report 2002.* London: Office of the e-Envoy. Available online (accessed 10 December 2003) at: http://www.e-envoy.gov.uk/Resources/AnnualReport2002/fs/en

e-Minister and e-Envoy (2002) *Monthly Report – 4 February 2002.* London: Office of the e-Envoy. Available online (accessed 10 December 2003) at: http://www.e-envoy.gov.uk/EStrategy/MonthlyReportsArticle/fs/ en?CONTENT_ID= 4000027&chk=IbRkf4

European Commission (2002a) *eEurope Action Plan 2002/ eAccessibility: WAI Contents Guidelines for Public Web Sites in the EU.* Available online (accessed 10 December 2003) at: http://europa.eu.int/ comm/employment_social/knowledge_society/eacc_wai.pdf

European Commission (2002b) *A Review of Legislation Relevant to Accessibility in Europe*. Available online (accessed 10 December 2003) at: http://europa.eu.int/comm/employment_social/knowledge_society/ eacc_rev_leg.pdf

European Parliament (2002) *eEurope 2002: Accessibility of Public Web Sites and Their Content*, Parliament Resolution (2002) 0325. Available online (accessed 10 December 2003) at: http://europa.eu.int/ information_society/topics/citizens/accessibility/web/wai_2002/ ep_res_web_wai_ 2002/index_en.htm

European Union (2003) Ministerial Symposium, declaration on eInclusion – 'Towards an Inclusive Information Society in Europe'. Available online (accessed 10 Dec 2003) at: http://www.eu2003.gr/en/ articles/2003/4/11/2502/index.asp?

Farrow, M. (2003) *The Internet Encourages Me to Create and Participate*. Washington, DC: National Organization on Disability. Available online (accessed 10 December 2003) at: http://www.nod.org/ content.cfm?id=1309

Grundy, E., Ahlburg, D., Ali, M., Breeze, E. and Sloggett, A. (1999) *Disability in Great Britain*, Research Report No. 94. London: DSS

Hall Aitken Associates (2002) *Evaluation of CMF-funded UK Online Centres: Initial Report*. Research Report RR368. London: DfES

Kingston, R. (2001) *The Social Implications of E-Commerce: A Review of Policy and Research*. York: Joseph Rowntree Foundation

Knight, J., Heaven, C. and Christie, I. (2002) *Inclusive Citizenship*. London: Leonard Cheshire

Mason, S. and Casserley, C. (2001) 'Web site design and the Disability Discrimination Act 1995', *Computers and Law*, Vol. 12, No. 5, pp. 16–20

NOD (National Organization on Disability) (2001) *Impact of the Internet on Community Participation*, NOD/Harris Survey. Summary available online (accessed 10 December 2003) at: http://www.nod.org/ content.cfm?id=139

Oftel (2000) *Consumers' Use of Internet.* Summary of Oftel residential survey, June 2000. Available online (accessed 9 March 2004) at: http://www.ofcom.org.uk/static/archive/oftel/publications/research/int0800.htm

Oftel (2002) *Consumers' Use of Internet.* Oftel residential survey Q8 February 2002. Available online (accessed 24 February 2004) at: http://www.ofcom.org.uk/static/archive/oftel/publications/research/2002/q8intr0402.htm

Oftel (2003) *Consumers' Use of Internet.* Oftel residential survey Q11 November 2002 – January 2003. Available online (accessed 24 February 2004) at: http://www.ofcom.org.uk/static/archive/oftel/publications/research/2003/q11intr0103.htm

ONS (2001a) *Internet Access, 26 September 2001.* London: National Statistics

ONS (2001b) *Internet Access, 18 December 2001.* London: National Statistics

ONS (2002) *Internet Access, 17 December 2002.* London: National Statistics. Also available online (accessed 10 December 2003) at: http://www.statistics.gov.uk/pdfdir/inta1202.pdf

ONS (2003) 'Adults who have accessed the Internet by purpose of Internet use (for personal use): individual Internet access'. Available online (accessed 10 December 2003) at: http://www.statistics.gov.uk/StatBase/xsdataset.asp?More=Y&vlnk=4089&All=Y&B2.x=62&B2.y=6)

Pahl, J. (1999) *Invisible Money: Family Finances in the Electronic Economy.* Bristol: The Policy Press in association with the Joseph Rowntree Foundation

Pilling, D. (1997) *The Computerised Information and Guidance Project (Now Called GROW, Gateways to Reaching Opportunities for Work),* Evaluation Report to DfEE. London: Rehabilitation Resource Centre, City University

Porter, P. (1997) 'The reading washing machine', *Vine*, Vol. 106, pp. 34–7

Research Surveys of Great Britain (2001) *ICT Access and Use: Report on the Benchmark Survey*, Research Report No. 252. London: DfES. Also available (accessed 10 December 2003) at: www.dfes.gov.uk/research/data/uploadfiles/RR252.doc

RNIB (2002) *Get the Picture. Making Television Accessible to Blind and Partially Sighted People.* London: RNIB

Russell, N. and Stafford, N. (2002) *Trends in ICT Access and Use*, Research Report No. 358. London: DfES. Available online (accessed 10 December 2003) at: www.dfes.gov.uk/research/data/uploadfiles/RR358.doc

US Congress (1990) *Americans with Disabilities Act 1990*. Text of the ADA, Public Law 336 of the 101st Congress, enacted 26 July 1990. Available online (accessed 10 December 2003) at: http://www.usdoj.gov/crt/ada/pubs/ada.txt

US Congress (1998) *Rehabilitation Act 1973, Section 508 Amendment (1998)*. Guidelines and other relevant legislation available online (accessed 10 December 2003) at: www.section508.gov

WAI (Web Accessibility Initiative) (2002) Websites accessed (10 December 2003): www.w3.org and www.w3.org/wai/

Glossary

Accessibility

The ability of goods, services and locations to be obtained, used or reached by all people with different individual needs and preferences. This report highlights issues of accessibility concerning computer operation and Internet-deliverable services for people with disabilities. However, accessibility is important to all people, whether or not they currently have disabilities. The same accessibility features often provide varying benefits to more than one group of people: one group may gain in convenience or ease of use, for example, while another group may find such features essential for basic use of the product or service.

Access to Work (AtW)

A government scheme which provides advice, information and grants towards any extra employment costs that result from disability. It can help to pay for a support worker, special aids and equipment (which would include assistive devices to enable an employee to use a computer), and adaptations to existing premises and equipment. Help is obtainable by contacting the nearest AtW Business Centre.

Assistive device

An item of equipment or a software program which serves to increase or maintain a person's functional abilities in order to use a personal computer or services obtainable through the computer (such as on the Internet).

Bobby accessibility checking tool

A tool with which to assess an Internet website's level of accessibility – see http://www.cast.org/bobby.

Braille

A system of text communication for people with visual impairments by which text forms are designated by raised dot patterns, readable by touch.

Chatroom

An Internet website facility (usually needing special software) by which people can choose to participate in a live text conversation with others who seek that website and volunteer to take part in a 'chat' online.

Disability Discrimination Act (DDA)

The 1995 Act of Parliament which introduced new measures aimed at ending discrimination faced by many disabled people. It protects disabled people in the areas of employment, education and access to goods, facilities and services. The Special Educational Needs and Disability Act (SENDA) of 2001 removed exclusions in education and amended Part IV of the DDA to require schools, colleges, universities and providers of adult education and youth services to ensure that they do not discriminate against disabled people.

Disability Rights Commission

An independent body (established by Parliament in 1999) to eliminate discrimination against disabled people and promote equality of opportunity. Its specific tasks include: advice and information service for disabled people, employers and service providers; problem-solving by negotiation and the Disability Conciliation Service; events, conferences and campaigns to raise public awareness of disability issues; policy statements and research on issues which affect disabled people.

Email

A system of sending and receiving messages between Internet-connected parties by means of special software. Email is closely analogous to sending and receiving communications by post, but accomplished electronically. Email is not 'live' but consists of recorded messages sent between computers.

Hal

A commercial product name for screen-reading software, generating speech or Braille versions of anything on a computer screen (with a computer sound card or a Braille device); like Supernova (see below), available from Dolphin Computer Access.

Home page

The entry point of an Internet website – the starting point of the website's information from which the other contents of the website can be located.

Instant Messaging

A system of sending and receiving instantaneous text messages between specific individuals who are connected online at the same time and who have special software with which to effect the contact. Unlike chatrooms (see above), Instant Messaging is an individual person-to-person communication in which each party waits for the other party to write his/her side of the 'conversation' through the computer as a 'live' process.

Internet

The international communal system of connectedness between computers by which data is available for sending and receiving, subject to computer programs' ability to facilitate the connections and to commercially controlled access points to connect to the network.

Javascript

A computer programming language which, like another language called Java, has features which can be used to help create programs that have good accessibility.

JAWS

A commercial product name acronym, standing for Job Access for Windows Software, made by an American company called Freedom Scientific. JAWS is a popular screen reader, a program which converts text to speech, of particular use to people with visual impairments.

Joystick

A lever that moves in all directions and controls the movement of a pointer or some other display symbol on a computer screen. A joystick can be designed to be used instead of a mouse. Conventionally (unless adapted otherwise), its main difference from a mouse is that whereas a mouse-controlled cursor stops moving as soon as you stop moving the mouse, with a joystick the pointer continues moving in the direction the joystick is pointing; to stop the pointer, you must return the joystick to its upright position. Most joysticks include trigger buttons, which operate like the clickable buttons on a mouse.

Learndirect

A government-sponsored network of work skills-related online learning and information services, developed by a public/private partnership organisation, University for Industry. Over 80 per cent of the courses are online, others are delivered on CD-ROM and there are some workbook-based courses.

Markup

A textual description of data which designates its appearance – such as underlinings, italics and paragraph breaks in text.

Navigation

The pursuit of a particular route or course through Internet websites (as opposed to 'browsing' or 'surfing' which are undetermined wanderings through Internet websites).

Newsgroup

A message board available through the Internet by which people sharing an interest can read, place and reply to messages from one another.

Oftel

The abbreviation for the Office of Telecommunications which was the regulator for the UK telecommunications industry until the end of 2003. From 2004 its tasks and duties have become those of Ofcom, the Office of Communications, which also now regulates television and radio. The Offices promote and protect the interests of consumers, maintain and promote effective competition and ensure that telecommunications services are provided in the UK to meet all reasonable demands.

Online

Being connected to the Internet.

Screen reader

A software program which enables a computer user to listen to a synthetic voice description of screen displays of text or images and icons (provided they have text descriptions when designed). Mostly used by visually impaired people, screen readers also typically perform organising or reformatting tasks when working on web pages, in order to convert complicated visual material into a navigable vocal form.

Speech recognition/voice recognition/voice-activated

Software which works in conjunction with a microphone connected to a computer equipped with a sound card in order to enable a computer user to generate written text directly from speaking the words (instead of typing in the words on a keyboard), or to enable him or her to operate the computer in various ways (such as moving between programs or working on files).

Supernova

A commercial product name for software which magnifies computer screens, generates speech for computer operation or helps (with additional equipment) to generate Braille versions of visual information; like Hal (see above), available from Dolphin Computer Access.

Tag

A type of programming command or instruction within the 'coding' of a web page which designates some aspect of appearance such as a paragraph break or bold type in a text page or, in the case of 'text tag explanation', which designates a text description of a visual image which screen-reading software can read out aloud to the computer user.

U Can Do It

A charity which provides computer training for blind, deaf and disabled people in their own homes; their basic course consists of ten training sessions and includes email, surfing the web and an introduction to newsgroups and chatrooms.

UK online centre

A location where computers with Internet access are available at low cost to enable people to use or train on 'new technology' skills and equipment. The locations include Internet cafés on shopping streets, public libraries, colleges, community centres, or anywhere else available to the public. UK online centres are a government initiative intended to meet the needs of local people who have low or no ICT skills (skills in information and communication technology). Training assistance, assistive devices and physical access to UK online centres vary between centres.

University for Industry

A public/private partnership organisation which operates in England, Wales and Northern Ireland to provide work-related training courses under the banner of learndirect.

Unmetered access

Connection to the Internet through an 'Internet Service Provider' for a flat subscription fee, unrestricted by a connection time limit.

User interface

The way in which a system presents itself to, and interacts with, a human user.

W3C – World Wide Web Consortium

An international Internet and computing industry consortium founded in 1994 to develop common protocols and promote the web's evolution, ensuring that newly developing web capabilities can be accessed and used on all different types of computers.

WAI – Web Accessibility Initiative

A set of policy actions by W3C (see above), following collaboration with disability organisations, research centres and governments, which has resulted in widely accepted guidelines to improve web accessibility for disabled people.

Windows

The commercial brand name of an operating system produced by America's Microsoft Corporation which dominates the personal computer market. The operating system is the main operating program of a computer – it manages and interacts with all the other programs on a computer, called applications, which carry out specific tasks.

Zoomtext

A commercial product name for software which magnifies, enhances or reads aloud from computer screens; made by Ai Squared.

Appendix: The questionnaire survey

Can the Internet be more useful for disabled people?

The Internet has surged in general popularity in the last few years, but is it usable and useful or entertaining for disabled people?

Do we get enough out of it? Could we? Do we want to?

Please help us find the facts with this questionnaire – it's research by City University (London), funded by the Joseph Rowntree Foundation. **We are equally interested in your views if you are an Internet user, or if you've never used the Internet or no longer do so.**

The Internet is like an electronic skeleton! But the flesh and bones are the uses we make of it. Biggest uses of it up to now are surfing the so-called World Wide Web (used for information and shopping), email (notes and letters whizzing electronically instead of via the postman) and Chat and Instant Messaging ('chatrooms', ICQ, Microsoft Messenger, Yahoo Messenger, etc.) where people can have instantaneous 'live' conversations and newsgroups (for non-live exchanges).

We're finding out if and how disabled people use the Internet. Are there difficulties and frustrations? Can they be overcome? Is there anything special you want from the Internet?

THE INFORMATION YOU GIVE US WILL BE TREATED IN STRICT CONFIDENCE AND YOUR INDIVIDUAL DETAILS WILL NOT BE PASSED ON TO ABILITYNET OR ANY OTHER ORGANISATION

To make the questionnaire easy to fill in we have included boxes to tick, but please feel free to give us any other information you wish.

Please send us your answers in the FREEPOST envelope. For further information, or if you'd prefer questions by phone, by email, or in Braille, please ring Doria Pilling on 020 8992 4302 or email her at d.s.pilling@city.ac.uk or fill in the tear-off slip below and post it to us.

FILL THIS IN IF YOU'D PREFER ANOTHER METHOD OF ANSWERING
I would prefer to answer:

☐ **Over the telephone**   ☐ **By email**
☐ **In Braille**   ☐ **By textphone**

Name ....

(Text)Phone no ....   email address ....

Disabled people and the Internet

SECTION A

1. **Have you ever accessed the Internet, this includes using email, World Wide Web, Instant Messaging (*), newsgroups, chatrooms or any other use?**

    ☐ Yes **please go to question 2.**
    ☐ No **please go to Section D**

(*) ICQ, Microsoft Messenger, Yahoo Messenger, AOL Messenger, etc.

2. **When did you first use the Internet for these activities?**

	Never used it for this activity	Within the last month	More than 1 month ago, but less than 1 year ago	More than 1 year ago, but less than 3 years ago	More than 3 years ago
Email					
World Wide Web					
Chat					
Instant Messaging (*)					
Newsgroups					
Others					

(*) ICQ, Microsoft Messenger, Yahoo Messenger, AOL Messenger, etc.

3. **When did you last use the Internet for these activities?**

	Never used it for this activity	In the last 7 days	Over a week ago, up to a month	Over a month ago, up to 3 months	Over 3 months ago, up to 6 months	Over 6 months ago
Email						
World Wide Web						
Chat						
Instant Messaging (*)						
Newsgroups						
Others						

(*) ICQ, Microsoft Messenger, Yahoo Messenger, AOL Messenger, etc.

If you ticked 'Others' in question 2 and 3, please specify:.............................
....
....

4.   **Have you used any of the above Internet activities for the following purposes? Please tick all purposes that apply.**

☐ Private or personal use   ☐ Further education college university
☐ Work   ☐ Other educational or training course
☐ School   ☐ Other (please specify) ....

5a.   **Do you need special aids/equipment or adaptations to enable you to use a computer generally or the Internet?**

☐ Yes   (Please specify): ....
....
....

☐ No

5b.   **Have you had any problems about lack of availability of the special aids, equipment or adaptation that you need to use a computer or the Internet? Please indicate the locations in which these have occurred by ticking the appropriate boxes below:**

	Lack of availability of special aids of equipment or adaptations	Insufficient support
My own home		
My workplace		
A school		
Further education college/university		
Public library		
Internet café or shop		
Community or voluntary organisation		
Somewhere else (Please specify)		

Please tell us about the problems you have experienced: ....
....
....

6a. How did you learn to use the Internet?

Please tick all the methods that apply.

- ☐ Self-taught, using Help or on-line tutorials *only*
- ☐ Self-training, using tutorials, written, on tape or CD
- ☐ From a friend or relative
- ☐ From colleague/s at work
- ☐ On a training course

If you have been on an Internet training course please go to question 6b, if not go to question 6f.

6b. Did you take an Internet training course on your own initiative or was it in relation to your work?

- ☐ Own initiative
- ☐ Work

6c. Where did you obtain this training?

....

....

....

6d. Have you any comments about how this training could have been improved?

....

....

....

6e. **Please tick the boxes below to indicate what training was provided and how useful it was**

	Training provided		Usefulness		
	Yes	No	Very useful	Useful	Not very useful
Searching the Web					
Downloading files					
Sending and receiving email					
Online shopping					
Use of chatrooms					
Use of Instant Messaging applications (*)					
Use of any special aids/equipment or adaptations					
Web design					
Other (Please specify)					

(*) ICQ, Microsoft Messenger, Yahoo Messenger, AOL Messenger, etc.

Please go to question 7a.

6f. **If you have not taken an Internet training course, would you have liked to?**

☐ Yes **please go to question 6g**
☐ No **please go to question 7a**
☐ Not sure/don't know **please go to question 7a**

6g. **If you would have liked training, what were the problems in obtaining this? Please tick all that apply.**

☐ Finding course in my locality
☐ Disabled access
☐ Facilities for people with sensory or other impairments
☐ Cost
☐ Other (please specify): ....
....
....

Please comment on any difficulties you have had in finding suitable training

....

....

....

....

7a. **If you have used the World Wide Web, what do you think in general about most sites? Please tick the statement that best fits your views:**

☐ I have never used the Web   **please go to question 8a**
☐ Most websites are easy to understand and get around
☐ Many websites are easy to understand and get around
☐ Some websites are easy to understand and get around
☐ Only a few websites are easy to understand and get around

7b. **Can you suggest any ways in which web sites could be better designed for easier use?**

....

....

....

8a. **Would you like to use the Internet more than you do at present?**

☐ Yes   **please go to question 8b**
☐ No   **please go to question 8d**

8b. **What are the main reasons preventing you from using the Internet more? Please tick all the reasons that apply.**

☐ Cost of buying own computer
☐ Difficulty in obtaining advice/information on special aids/equipment that I need
☐ Cost of buying special aids/equipment that I need
☐ Lack of availability of aids/equipment that I need in many locations
☐ Lack of knowledge of how to install Internet access at home
☐ Cost of online access at home
☐ Cost of online access at locations outside home
☐ Other (please specify): ....

....

Have you any additional comments on this issue?

....

....

....

8c. What would you most like to use the Internet more for?

....

....

....

8d. If you would not like to use the Internet more than you do at present, what are the reasons for this?

....

....

....

If you use/have used the Internet for your personal or private use, please go to section B. If not go to Section E.

SECTION B

Complete this section if you use or have used the Internet for your **PERSONAL OR PRIVATE** use. If not, please move to section E.

9. Thinking about when you access the Internet for your personal or private use, how often do/did you usually access the Internet?

☐ At least once a day
☐ Several times a week
☐ Once a week
☐ Once or twice a month
☐ Less than once a month

10a. Which of these places have you used to access the Internet for your personal or private use? Please tick all locations that you use/have used.

☐ My own home
☐ Another person's home
☐ My workplace
☐ School
☐ College, university or other educational or training institution
☐ Public library
☐ Government office
☐ Internet café or shop
☐ Community or voluntary organisation
☐ Post office
☐ Somewhere else (please specify): ....

....

10b. Which of these places do you use MOST to access the Internet for your personal or private use?

....

....

....

10c. What are the reasons for using this place the most for Internet access?

....

....

....

11a. Thinking about when you use the Internet for your personal or private use, for which of these activities have you accessed the Internet? Please tick all that apply.

- [ ] Using email
- [ ] Finding information about goods and services (including holidays, flights, houses)
- [ ] Buying or ordering tickets/goods/services
- [ ] Personal banking, financial and investment activities
- [ ] Looking for jobs or work
- [ ] Downloading software, including games
- [ ] Playing or downloading music
- [ ] Finding information related to schoolwork or an educational course
- [ ] Using or accessing government/official services
- [ ] General browsing or surfing
- [ ] Other things (please specify): ....

....

....

....

11b. Which of these activities do you use the Internet for most?

....

....

....

11c. What are the advantages of using the Internet for these activities?

....

....

....

11d. How did you carry out these activities before you had use of the Internet?

....

....

....

11e. If you do not buy or order goods or services over the Internet, what is the main reason for this?

....

....

....

11f. What are the main reasons for not using the Internet for any of the other activities listed above?

....

....

....

12. Overall, what do you see as the main advantages in using the Internet?

....

....

....

13. Overall, what are the disadvantages in using the Internet?

....

....

....

If you are or have been able to access the Internet at home please go on to Section C, if not please go to Section E.

SECTION C

For those who are/have been able to access the Internet from home.

14a. **By what means do/did you access the Internet from home? Please tick all that apply.**

- ☐ Own computer
- ☐ Someone else's computer
- ☐ Digital TV
- ☐ Mobile/WAP phone
- ☐ Games console
- ☐ Other (please specify): ....
....

14b. **Which of these means of access do you usually use?**

....
....
....

15a. **From where did you obtain help/information in initially accessing the Internet at home?**

....
....
....

15b. **Was this help/information adequate?**

....
....
....

15c. **Would you have liked additional help? What kind of additional help would you have liked?**

....
....
....

16. Did you encounter any problems when you initially tried to access the Internet from home? Please describe any problems and whether and how these were overcome.

....

....

17. Do you still have any problems in accessing the Internet from home?

☐ Yes (please specify): ....

....

....

☐ No

Please go on to Section E

SECTION D

For those who have never used the Internet.

18. Please tell us why you have never used the Internet.

....

....

....

19. If you have a computer at home, but do not have, or do not use Internet access, please tell us why this is.

....

....

....

20. If you do not have a computer at home, or are unable to use a computer at home, please give us the reasons for this.

....

....

....

21. Is there anything that would make it more likely that you would use the Internet in the future? Please tell us about it.

....

....

....

22.	**If you would like to use the Internet, what would you most like to use it for?**

☐ Using email (sending letters and notes to friends and family)
☐ Using chat rooms (communicating with people having the same interests as you)
☐ Instant Messaging (having a real-time conversation using text with friends, family, colleagues, etc.)
☐ Finding information about goods and services (including holidays, flights, houses, timetables, etc.)
☐ Buying or ordering tickets, goods, services, etc.
☐ Personal banking, financial and investment activities
☐ Looking for jobs or work
☐ Downloading software
☐ Playing games
☐ Playing or downloading music
☐ Gambling
☐ Finding information related to schoolwork or an educational course
☐ Using or accessing government/official services
☐ Other things (please specify): ....

....

....

SECTION E

For everyone

23a.	**Have you heard of the government's UK Online Campaign**

☐ Yes
☐ No

23b.	**Do you know where your local UK online centre is?**

☐ Yes
☐ No

23c.	**Do you think it a good idea for the government to make all its services available online?**

☐ Yes
☐ No

Please give us your views:

....

....

....

24. **Are you:**

- ☐ Male
- ☐ Female

25. **Which age group are you in?**

- ☐ Under 16
- ☐ 16–19
- ☐ 20–24
- ☐ 25–34
- ☐ 35–44
- ☐ 45–54
- ☐ 55–64
- ☐ 65 and over

26. **How would you describe your disability?**

....
....
....

27. **How does your disability affect your use of computers?**

....
....
....

28. **For how long have you been disabled?**

....
....
....

29. **Which of the following best describes your situation? Please tick one statement only.**

- ☐ In full-time paid employment
- ☐ In part-time paid employment
- ☐ Unemployed, looking for work
- ☐ Looking after home or family
- ☐ Unable to work at the moment because of illness or disability
- ☐ Retired
- ☐ At school
- ☐ At college/university

☐ On training scheme
☐ Doing voluntary work
☐ Other (please specify): ....

....

....

....

30a. **If you are/have been in paid work, what is/was your usual occupation?**

....

....

....

30b. **If you are not working now, how long ago did you leave your last job?**

☐ Less than 6 months ago
☐ 6 months to 1 year ago
☐ 1–2 years ago
☐ 2–3 years ago
☐ 3+ years ago

31. **Do you have any other comments on the use of the Internet that haven't been addressed in this questionnaire?**

Name ....

If you would not mind us contacting you if we need to clarify any issues please give us your:

– Telephone (textphone) number: ....

– or your email address: ....

Would you be willing to take part in a discussion about using the Internet?

☐ Yes   ☐ No

THANK YOU VERY MUCH FOR YOUR HELP

Please send the completed questionnaire to us in the FREEPOST envelope provided